# All My Dogs

FOR LULU

# All My Dogs

## A LIFE

BILL HENDERSON

*drawings by* LESLIE MOORE

DAVID R. GODINE, *Publisher*
BOSTON

First published in 2011 by
DAVID R. GODINE · *Publisher*
Post Office Box 450
Jaffrey, New Hampshire 03452
*www.godine.com*

LIBRARY OF CONGRESS
CATALOGING-IN-PUBLICATION DATA
Henderson, Bill, 1941–
All my dogs: a life / by Bill Henderson; illustrated by Leslie Moore.
p.    cm.
ISBN 978-1-56792-435-0
1. Dogs—Anecdotes.  2. Dog owners—Anecdotes.  3. Dog owners—
Biography.  4. Henderson, Bill, 1941–   5. Human-animal
relationships – Anecdotes.   I. Title.
SF426.2.H46 2011
636.70092'9—dc22
2010049824

First edition 2011
Printed in the United States of America

# Contents

Inscription on the monument of a
Newfoundland dog (1808):
*Near this spot are deposited the remains of one who possessed Beauty without Vanity, Strength without Insolence, Courage without Ferocity, and all the Virtues of Man without his Vices. This Praise, which would be unmeaning Flattery if inscribed over human ashes, is but a just tribute to the Memory of Boatswain, a Dog.*
LORD BYRON

*I am because my little dog knows me.*
GERTRUDE STEIN

*A dog is the only thing on earth that loves you more than you love yourself.*
JOSH BILLINGS

# Prelude

A FEW YEARS AGO my dog Lulu and I were diagnosed with cancer. Mine was caught early and is being treated. For her it was too late.

We had spent ten years together, after I had found her abandoned at the local animal shelter – ten years of waking and sleeping. We were almost never apart. She was a being of enormous dignity, grace, and affection. To lose her was devastating. Of the many dogs I have known, she was my life dog, the one closest to my heart.

Like all of us who lose a friend, we seek to remember them. This little book is my tribute to Lulu and to all the wonderful dogs who instructed me in my almost seventy years.

It is also a tribute to the people I have met, especially

my parents, my wife, and our child Holly. Dogs and humans share this memoir equally, a curious hybrid, a mutt memoir if you will.

Memoirs of dogs and their people have a long history. In 1936, Elizabeth von Arnim, an admired wit and literary figure of her day, published *All the Dogs of My Life*, which was part autobiography and also an account of the many dogs she loved and occasionally loathed during her life in Germany, Switzerland, London, and the French Riviera. It may have been the first instance of the modern dog/human memoir.

My modest life in Philadelphia, New York, Long Island, and Maine was not that of Mrs. von Arnim. In fact, she died the year I was born (1941), having been married to a German count, given birth to five children, entertained stellar friends like her lover H. G. Wells and her cousin Katherine Mansfield, and endured a later and disastrous (dogless) marriage to Bertrand Russell's brother Frank. At the outbreak of World War II, she moved to America and died as I was starting out.

Her many and varied dogs were named Bijou, Bildad, Cornelia, Ingraham, Ingulf, Iago, Ivo, Prince, Coco, Pincher, Knobbie, Chunkie, Woosie, and Winkie. While she honored her dogs with names, most of the humans in her memoir were not named, not worth it.

My dogs have been called Trixie, Duke, Snopes, Ellen, Rocky, Sophie, Charlie, Airport, Opie, Lulu, Max, St. Francis of Assisi (Franny), and Sedgwick: all sizes, shapes, breeds, and mixes. With them, through them, and beside them I have grown from a five-year-old boy to my present perspective.

This personal memoir honors all of them, even those

I had disagreements with. I never could live without dogs, at least not well. In my dogless years I was busy and ambitious but half alive.Why can't I live well without dogs? Probably if you have read this far (and are not exclusively a cat lover) you can't either and can help answer the question for me. It is about steady, honest, and unconditional love – which is the virtue of many faiths, both secular and traditional – which is why I stay close to my dogs and my faith.

Do I have favorites of my thirteen dogs? I do. Lulu and many others – but that will become apparent. Just to name them gets me to blubbering. The problem with dogs is – and it's so unfair – they live such short lives. We, on the other hand, the often unworthy, are here for such a very long time, in perpetual mourning for our lost friends.

Sorrow drives some readers away from the dog memoir. Dogs die, as Jon Katz notes in *The Dogs of Bedlam Farm*, and readers object. Why? We read biographies of great and noble people. They all expire. But somehow it hurts more when a great dog dies. I miss both people and dogs and long to talk with them again. But I can't. So I honor them in words and attempt to hold on to what they brought to me.

The dog memoir has seen many wonderful titles since von Arnim's – J. R. Ackerley's *My Dog Tulip* (1956), Farley Mowat's *The Dog Who Wouldn't Be* (1957), Ted Kerasote's *Merle's Door* (2005), John Grogan's *Marley & Me* (2005), and Mark Doty's *Dog Years* (2007) to name but a few of my favorites, genre classics all, I think.

In many of these memoirs, the dog is the heart of the family – be it two people or an extended household. The dog offers the author what any good family member would, love and guidance and solace, and the author grows spiritually with the dog. Jon Katz points out, "For some people, dogs and other animals are the only beings they can trust. Dogs show them it's OK to love again, no matter the trauma or mistreatment they have suffered. Sometimes, dogs show them the way back."

In *Marley & Me*, John Grogan comments,

*A person can learn a lot from a dog, even a loopy one like ours . . . Marley taught me about living each day with unbridled exuberance and joy, about seizing the moment and following your heart. He taught me to appreciate the simple things – a walk in the woods, a fresh snowfall, a nap in a shaft of winter sunlight. And as he grew old and achy, he taught me about optimism in the face of adversity.*

Many of my dogs taught me well too. Most of all they created home for me. From Philadelphia's suburbs to the Maine seaside, home was where the dog was. In the years when I was dogless, I had no true home. In the golden dog days, I found family again.

To me a good family is everything, as close to heaven as we are likely to get on earth. Dogs can help take us there.

This then is a book about dogs but also about family, marriage, and the birth of a wonderful child. Most of all it is about love and about how love finds us and how lucky we are when it does.

# Trixie

*The dog was created specially for children.*
*He is the god of Frolic.*
HENRY WARD BEECHER

EARLY IN THE EVENING of March 10, 1965, my father knelt by his bed, said his prayers, covered up, and slept forever. Not long after, Trixie too died in her sleep. My mother, still devastated from Pop's sudden death, found Trixie in her bed under the Formica-covered kitchen table. Stiff, quiet at last. She was seventeen.

Trixie was my first dog. She guided me through a childhood of suburban comfort and spiritual terror. Back in the 1940s, we lived in a tiny and tidy house in a tiny and tidy suburb just across Philadelphia's city line called Penn Wynne. When I was seven, my brother, sister, and I had begged Mom and Pop for a dog, and on Christmas morning 1948, we got Trixie, a purchase, a gift, a rescue from the pound, we never knew. Perhaps she had been unloaded by someone sick of the Germans – Trixie was a German spitz mix puppy.

In 1948, horror was all about us. The German descent into unspeakable savagery was still being revealed. The Russians were about to join us with the Bomb. It seemed sheer madness had seized the human creature.

Our parents shielded us from the worst of this news, but we sensed the enveloping fear around us. Trixie, the German spitz, was of course innocent of human insanity, as most dogs are, unless driven insane by their masters.

Trixie was an odd name in our devout family. It suggested bawdiness, perhaps a striptease dancer or a nightclub singer, associations that would have upset my parents. But perhaps they thought they owed it to the dog to keep her name. So Trixie it was for all of her laughing years.

If there was a depression of Spirit in the world, Trixie refused to join in. After all, her spitz ancestors went back a bit – European spitz-type dogs had been around for more than 6,000 years as hunters, herders, and watchdogs. The modern breed came in two sizes – small and medium. Trixie was the medium, about thirty pounds, mostly white with black spots here and there, a foxy face, up-pricked ears, and a bushy tail that curled over her back in a grand flourish. She was a superior watchdog, was interested in just about everything, and all of her life until the very end, she loved to play.

In a childhood that often hung over me gently like a

wet coat of do's and don'ts and admonitions to pray without ceasing, Trixie let me know it was also OK to play without ceasing– in fact, it was just fine to play until you dropped.

Like all children, I was yet to be dominated by words. Trixie and I were blessedly wordless together. As Virginia Woolf observed about Flush, a cocker spaniel, "Not a single one of his myriad sensations ever submitted itself to the deformity of words."

Play was Trixie's God. In the beginning was Play. Her worship demanded only that she diligently chase her hard, black rubber ball. She and I worshipped daily from an overstuffed blue couch. I tossed her ball into the corners of our tiny living room and Trixie retrieved it, jumped on the couch, made me wrestle the ball from her mouth, and set off when I threw it again. As we played and wrestled in German spitz joy, I seldom realized the deadly and growing seriousness of my seven-year-old life.

⊰ At our Penn Wynne breakfasts, Mom squeezed oranges for fresh juice, dosed us with cod liver oil, mixed the Ovaltine, and cooked hot Wheatena. At our feet, Trixie devoured her canned Ken-L Ration from a shiny metal bowl. Sitting next to Ruth in her highchair, Pop spooned his cereal and listened intently to Reverend Carl McIntire's *Twentieth-Century Reformation Hour* on the Philco radio. Reverend McIntire shouted that the Communists were advancing across Europe and the Russians would soon have the A-bomb, and that meant the End was near just as predicted in Revelation: "Blessed are those who wash their robes, that they may have the right to the tree of life and that they may enter the city by the gates. Outside are the dogs and sorcerers and fornicators and murderers and idolaters."

Reverend McIntire's words – even the few I understood – didn't scare me, and neither did his sadistic frenzy. My pop knew Reverend McIntire's God and what that God required of us. Pop and God would see that we were on the right side in the coming terror. The rule for kids was "Be Good."

Mother, who liked just about everybody – and was liked in return – treated everybody as if they were good: the Degger's Dairy milkman, the Freihofer's bread man, the teachers, the minister, most of the neighbors. Pop, in his short breakfast grace murmured under Reverend McIntire's shrieks, would often include Harry Truman in his list of good, God-fearing men.

Reverend McIntire raged through the breakfasts of my childhood. Everywhere I saw evidence of the End he predicted.

In the summer, Mom and we three kids escaped Carl McIntire's radio program in our Ocean City, New Jersey, summer cottage. Pop worked for General Electric in Philadelphia and joined us only on weekends, when McIntire was silent. In Ocean City, the government warned us that enemy subs lurked off the coast and we had to draw black window shades at night to block the light and confuse the infidels.

I picked up a newspaper from the front steps and ran inside shouting the headline to prove I could read such profundities: "War in Korea!"

One bright summer day, Mom, Trixie, and we children were walking the boardwalk when a Navy propeller fighter roared in from the sea, U-turned, and crashed suddenly just beyond the breakers. The pilot climbed from his cockpit and stood on the wing until lifeguards rowed out and rescued him.

"Why did the plane crash?" I asked Mother later. She said she didn't know, and I was baffled and scared. There had to be a reason for everything, didn't there? Sin of some sort caused the plane crash, I figured. That's what Pop might have said, but he was away at work.

To Pop, sin was real. Sin was the reason for everything terrible. Heaven and hell were actual places. Jesus and God were people who lived with us, not just pleasant suburban abstractions. The events of the world and of our every day were crammed with meaning and grand purpose.

Pop, who was as shy as he was kind, did not speak directly about such matters. He let Reverend McIntire do that. When my instructor, McIntire, complained as he often did that he was too poor, that the devil was at the door and he couldn't possibly continue his radio ministry unless all his listeners rushed him money, I wrote, "Dear Dr. McIntire, my name is Bill and my dog is Trixie and I am in bed with measles. I like your program. Here is twenty-five cents. This is my allowance. I will send you another twenty-five cents next week."

Reverend McIntire read my letter on the air and declared that it was most touching to receive this kind of widow's mite contribution from a bedridden child and his dog Trixie, and wouldn't God be pleased if everybody sacrificed like that. (Dogs, I realized from Revelation, wouldn't make it to heaven, but maybe Dr. McIntire was negotiating an exception for Trixie in gratitude for the twenty-five cents.)

He mailed me a purple plastic spoon "to feed the

gospel to the world" and a small, red velvet wall plaque that informed me in gold letters: "I can do all things through Christ which strengtheneth me. Philippians 4:13."

"All things," I wondered. I could do all things as long as I pleased Jesus by cleaning up my room, memorizing my Sunday School Bible verses, getting good report cards, and not picking my nose.

In Penn Wynne Elementary School I learned about the scary Permanent Record. This record was similar to God's heavenly record and to the less important records of Santa Claus and the Easter Bunny.

In third grade, the class watched the wonder of tadpoles changing into frogs. Most of the tadpoles had four legs and were just beginning to lose their tails, when Barry Lurton – a kid with the habit of grinning and simultaneously touching his tongue to the point of his nose – heaved the aquarium out of the second-floor window.

As we stood around the broken glass and almost frog bodies, our third-grade teacher tried to console us. "It wasn't Barry's fault," she said.

"Wasn't Barry's fault?" I wondered. Then whose fault was it?

Sure Barry was retarded, but it was still his fault.

Otherwise the deaths must be God's fault because God made Barry the way he was.

But that was unthinkable.

So I tried not to think. Instead I threw the hard rubber ball to Trixie, without ceasing.

Over the years, Trixie was ranked number one in a pack of a parakeets, canaries, hamsters, reptiles, and cats.

Boots the white-footed cat was second in rank– a pal to Trixie. They slept together in Trixie's bed until Boots was banished to a farm (I was told) because he slaughtered too many neighborhood birds and deposited them in the kitchen, perhaps as gifts to Trixie, who ignored their corpses.

In our Ocean City and Penn Wynne backyards, I cobbled together turtle pens from junk lumber and stocked them with diamondback terrapins from the Ocean City marshes and baby painted pond and box turtles from the fast-disappearing fields of Penn Wynne. My zoo grew to twelve turtles. Mom and I fed them leftover vegetables and Trixie's Ken-L Ration.

Once a schoolmate, the dastardly Hughie Barton from across the street, snuck past a sleeping Trixie in the middle of the night and stole a rare diamondback. Rather than confront him, I merely stole the turtle back the next night from Hughie's turtle pen, never mentioning it to Hughie, who acted as if nothing had happened.

In the winter, the turtles hibernated in the cellar with the snakes– a green snake and various garter snakes I kept in glass aquariums. One spring we stored a box of rattlesnakes in the garage– a favor to Bobby's second-grade teacher, Miss Dolan, who for some reason collected them. Miss Dolan also shot deer and squirrels, which she prepared for us in exotic dinners. When the rattlesnakes were in residence, we kids weren't allowed in the garage, but we thrilled when Trixie's bark inspired a chorus of indignant rattles, which Trixie enjoyed too. In a few months they were gone, back to the Pennsylvania woods where they originated. I never did figure out why they were stored with us that spring.

Trixie and her wordless pack kept me informed about another universe far from the theological threats and moral posturing of adults. Her pack did not deal in pathetic attempts at verbal definitions – a bark, meow, hiss, or rattle sufficed. They didn't twist themselves in knots of murderous argument about salvation, gender, race, or political creed. They were content to just be. To chase that black rubber ball and wrestle with me until my hands were red from her happy teeth was joy enough for Trixie.

≈§ In the evenings, Mother allowed us just one radio program: *Sergeant Preston of the Yukon and His Dog, King*, a serial about battling wickedness in the frozen north. Bobby and I sat on the living-room rug with our ears a few feet from the speaker. King, a German shepherd with an authoritative bark, was our superhero. We loved that dog as much as kids loved Superman or the Lone Ranger. We didn't know he was just a radio bark, perhaps didn't even exist. In our hearts he lived as much as, dare I say it, Jesus – at least at 5:30 P.M. he did.

When King was shot by claim jumpers – he howled awfully – and presumably was killed, Bobby and I collapsed in sobs and missed dinner. I was sick, wanted to throw up, but couldn't because I hadn't eaten anything. Mom tried to quiet me: "I'm certain King will be OK," she said, but I was beyond her solace.

Sure enough, King got better for the next evening's program. His bark was back. Mom baked a special cake for us to celebrate.

Late in the 1940s, Pop bought a gigantic secondhand television that, through a mirror, reflected images of Buster Crabbe, Bob Steele, Tom Mix, and Howdy Doody.

Later I watched the Army-McCarthy hearings on this TV and realized again that Carl McIntire had been right – something very important was happening in the world, but from this show it was hard to understand which side was God's: the Army's or McCarthy's.

I tossed the ball to Trixie and tried to forget about this puzzle.

Later in the evening we kids were given baths by Mother, who, as I grew older, instructed me to wash between my legs by myself, producing new mysteries. We dressed in our pajamas, climbed in bed, and Mother supervised evening prayers: "Now I lay me down to sleep. Pray the Lord my soul to keep. If I die before I wake . . ." I didn't know what a "layme" was, and the thought that I might die was ridiculous. If I had a cold or flu or worse, Pop would kneel by me with his hand on my head and pray that God make me better.

Every night I recited the Lord's Prayer and asked for blessings on our family and Trixie and all our animals and for my personal requirements such as help in remembering prepositions for an English quiz or penance for being bored in church or opening my eyes while praying or even thinking "damn" or accidentally ripping a page of a Bible or bumping a parent – the Bible said that parent-strikers were to be stoned to death without qualification – or disobeying any of the Ten Commandments, including the ones I didn't understand like, "Thou Shalt Not Covet Thy Neighbour's Wife, nor His Manservant . . . nor His Ass" (what did "covet" mean and wasn't "ass" a cussword?).

In every evening prayer I asked God to destroy all the bars in the world and replace each with a church. That was a priority request. Pop assured us that nothing was worse than a bar. His dad had been a raging drunk.

In the night while the drum-major music-box lamp played "Twinkle, Twinkle Little Star," my brother and I held hands between our beds. This was our insurance against the dreaded man in the attic or the dark presence in the cellar or the bogeyman lurking just outside our bedroom window in the lilac bush (the same bush that each spring filled our room with the fragrance of its blossoms).

A few steps down the hall, Mom and Pop read the Bible to each other and said their own prayers before sleeping. Their door was left open a crack so that Mother could hear our calls or cries. Once every night Ruth, Bobby, or I would ask her for a glass of water, and Mother, uncomplaining, would wake and bring the water. We were seldom really thirsty. We just wanted to be sure she was still there. Soothed, we would fall asleep again, listening to the distant clack-clack of the trolley to Philadelphia.

Downstairs Trixie kept the nightwatch.

Sundays at church it became simple again and then complicated all over. Our teachers were kindly ladies who propped up a board on an easel and, with felt silhouettes and landscapes, recited the most fabulous tales: about a wicked king who slaughtered all the male babies in an attempt to murder the Christ Child, about a wise king who offered to chop a baby in half to discover who its real mother was, and of course the appalling saga of young Isaac and his deranged dad Abraham who was about to sacrifice his son to the Lord until said Lord said, "That's OK, here's a ram." We were told this was an example of steadfast faith, a ghastly spin that has been repeated in sermons I've heard ever since.

We kids just listened and wondered and tried to forget what adults can do to kids.

These ladies told us more pleasant tales too: about Saul on the road to Damascus and the sudden light that led him to Jesus – such a light flooded the living room one day where Trixie and I played our ball game, and I knew Jesus had come to visit me and Trixie, that it wasn't just sunshine poking from behind a cloud.

Later in Sunday School I learned that I had not only sinned from time to time, but that I was a sinner.

"What do you mean we are all sinners? I'm not!" I cried out.

"Yes, you are, Billy. Every human is a sinner," said the teacher.

What was the use of even trying to be good if you ended up in the same category as real sinners certain to burn?

☙ In the summer the evangelists came to Ocean City. Billy Graham pitched a big tent in a gravel parking lot. I sat in the back of the tent on a wooden folding chair next to Pop and heard this new preacher shout from a platform decorated with potted palms about a Christian man who lapsed from the faith and began drinking and going with women. He stopped tithing and bought a Jaguar sports car with his tithing money. Finally God would not listen anymore to his prayers for forgiveness. The man parked his Jaguar on the Ben Franklin Bridge and jumped off.

At the end of the sermon, Billy asked all of us who wanted to be saved to raise our hands. I had thought I was saved from the day I put my hand on top of the radio, like Carl McIntire said to do, and said, "I believe." But as a convicted sinner you couldn't be too sure about such things. I didn't want to end up like the man who stopped tithing.

Billy pointed around the room, counting hands and acknowledging salvations. I leaned forward in my seat and waved my hand so that he wouldn't miss me, and I looked over at Pop. He smiled and nodded at me. I had pleased him greatly and I was glad.

For weeks afterward on our evening boardwalk strolls – surrounded by vacationers in shorts sucking on ice-cream cones and frozen custard, pushing baby carriages and trailing balloons, banging at pinball machines and blasting rifles at metal ducks– I felt exactly how I had been told I was supposed to feel. I was pounds lighter. My sins had been lifted from me. I was floating. I was certain that the crowd could see me floating.

"Saved!" I wanted to shout as we walked down the boardwalk toward home. And now Pop and I would save the whole world! This was a march, a march to banish sickness and pain and evil and war from the world and bring in Jesus Christ any day now. Holding Pop's hand with Trixie's leash in the other, I wanted to put my arms around everybody on the boardwalk.

But still the words had me worried. Was I really "saved"? Had the evangelist really seen my hand? It was a small hand. I was a small boy.

Poet Mark Doty, in his brilliant and moving *Dog Days*, comments that he grew up with apocalyptic parents "who believed the end was near, and that this phenomenal world was merely a veil soon to be torn away. This is great training for a lyric poet concerned with evanescence."

But all I got was uncertainty. I could never be sure of my contract with God. I wanted it in writing.

◆§ In sixth grade, the rational world (Trixie's) was even harder to hold on to. The school sponsored a weekly dancing class to teach us the social graces– how to dress nicely, speak properly, and cling to the opposite sex in a mannerly fashion. Dancing class was not an introduction to "sex." In those days even to say "sex" was risqué.

Pop was sure that dancing class was just as risqué. He forbade me from attending. But Mom overruled him. Thanks to Mom I learned how to fox trot, waltz, and long for and desperately fear girls.

Trixie announced "sex" to every visitor to our house. She had been spayed and for some reason the fur on her pelvis and crotch never grew back. She had been deprived of her right to bear children– that joy– and she had been disfigured. And she wasn't about to let us or any friend or stranger forget it. When they walked in the house, Trixie flopped over in their path and spread her legs and wouldn't move.

"Oh, she always does that," said Pop, chagrined as if Trixie were indeed the burlesque queen she may have been named for by her previous owner. "Trixie, get up!" Pop commanded. She never would. She testified to her damage until the visitor stepped over her, well informed about her complaint.

Despite her mutilation, Trixie was named "Best in Show" in the Penn Wynne Elementary School Pet Exhibition. She and I walked home together waving her blue ribbon, gushing in victory. (Gushing was another of

Pop's verbotens. Men of that era were supposed to be reserved.) Trixie gushed whenever she felt like it. She barked when it suited her, danced on her hind feet when asked, and charged around our house and yard possessed by her dog's wonder of each second. She was a supreme gusher. Years later I would remember that lesson from her – it was OK to dance and wonder and gush.

ᛋᚻ I was home for Pop's funeral when Trixie died. My mother, brother, sister, and I held a small ceremony for her and buried her in the backyard of our own new house in the fancier suburb of Bryn Mawr. I planted an oak sapling next to her grave, a tough tree for a tough spitz.

When Mom died in 1980, I inherited the blue couch that Trixie and I had played on. It was one of the few family items I kept, a memorial for Trixie and me and our ball games. I hauled that couch with me everywhere for years, to a cabin in the woods near Woodstock, New York, and finally to our home in East Hampton. It had become beat up, moldy, and mouse infested along the way. My wife and I moved it to the garage, where it sat abandoned for more years, becoming even moldier and more mouse ridden. Finally it seemed the couch was a health hazard. Sixty years after Trixie and I held our first ball game on that couch in 1948, I shoved it onto the roof of our car and deposited it in the "swap" area of the town dump, hoping somebody would discover virtue in its beaten form. Nobody did.

That evening I drove by the dump just in time to watch the bulldozer demolish the couch, smash it into a little pile. They loaded it with other trash and trucked it to a landfill upstate where it still is, at least in my imagination, a tribute to my first dog – the irrepressible German spitz hybrid with the saucy name who taught me it was just fine to play without ceasing.

# Duke

*Every boy should have two things: a dog and a
mother willing to let him have one.*
ANONYMOUS

I FIRST MET Duke at Walter Kuemerle's house. Walter
and I were both ten, friends from Penn Wynne Elementary School, where his dad taught shop class for boys
(girls took home economics). Like my dad, Mr. Kuemerle
was very handy. He showed us how to measure, saw,
screw, nail, solder, and weld – all the chores a boy of the
fifties should be able to do.

Walter and I hung out together after school many
afternoons at his house, about a mile from my place.
We'd hunt for crawfish, salamanders, frogs, and snakes
in a small creek nearby, then shoot hoops in his driveway.
When his dad bought one of the first new TVs in the
neighborhood (not used like ours and without the

reflecting mirror), we'd watch *Willy the Worm*, *Action in the Afternoon*, or *Ramar of the Jungle*, atrocious shows and a harbinger of what was to come. Then I'd head home on foot for dinner.

On the afternoon of October 3, 1951, Walter and I decided to check out the Giants–Dodgers playoff game. The winner would seize the National League championship. We didn't care who won – we were Phillies fans and now and then rooted for the Philadelphia A's. We popped two Pepsis and waited for the Dodgers to clinch it.

Up came the Giants' Bobby Thomson with two outs and two men on base. At 3:58 P.M. he smacked a homer, "the shot heard 'round the world" the papers would call it (borrowing a phrase from Emerson's poem about the Revolutionary War), and won the pennant for the Giants. Screams. Tears. Bedlam. The announcer at the Polo Grounds went berserk.

Next to the TV, Walter's new puppy, Butch, caught the fever and howled with the crowd, a Giants fan I presumed. Butch then tore around the den, upstairs and downstairs, and in utter abandon peed on Walter's dad's favorite chair.

That did it for Walter's dad, who had joined us to check out the noise. "That dog's gone tomorrow," our shop teacher announced.

Walter begged a reprieve. But Butch had snapped his dad's last synapse. It was the pound for Butch, and probably extermination, the next morning.

"Can I have him?" I meekly asked.

"Anything, just get him out of here. He's destroyed half the house."

Walter and I found a rope to fasten to Butch's collar. I promised Walter, who was morose, that he could visit

Butch anytime he wanted. It's like we'd share Butch. Anyway, he wouldn't be killed. Walter felt better after that. He hugged Butch good-bye, and off I set for my house, school books in one hand, Butch's rope in the other.

All the neighborhoods between Walter's home and mine were the same—two-story frame or brick houses on a quarter of an acre with a tree in the yard or maybe two and a one-car garage. They resembled the toy train villages in my Lionel collection: neat, clean, cramped, with that marvelous trickle of a creek running through it all—the trickle that Butch and I waded through as we began our life together and not far off Smith's Pond, a doomed swamp that would become our dream world.

I escorted Butch into the front door and called out to Mom in the kitchen, "Can I bring a friend home for dinner?"

"Sure," she called back gladly.

I'd gotten halfway to "yes" with her "sure," but the tough part was ahead. We already had that pen of turtles out back, a slither of snakes in the cellar, Boots the cat, Petie the canary, Pretty Boy the parakeet, and Trixie. Butch might be too much for Mom.

"Can I keep him? Walter gave him to me," I announced, rounding the kitchen corner. "They're maybe going to kill him tomorrow."

She sighed, thought it over for a few minutes, and then delivered the classic line of mom acquiescence: "only if you take care of him."

So Butch came to stay. Quickly he became Duke, because Butch sounded to me like a juvenile delinquent and I wanted a dignified dog; King was already taken.

Duke would indeed turn into nobility, even though he

was a thoroughbred mutt – some sort of spaniel mixed with whatever, springer spaniel I guessed because of his talent of jumping straight up and looking around for rabbits and pheasants at Smith's Pond. In a year he grew to forty-five pounds of white-and-black, floppy-eared, tick-collecting, field-romping primal force. (Trixie preferred to hunt indoors and avoided the exertion of the fields. The black ball you could at least catch, she knew. Duke never caught anything.)

At Smith's Pond, Duke began to teach me what I'd need to remember and would forget and remember again decades later.

Smith's Pond was the last hint of wilderness in Penn Wynne, no cute lawns and asphalt driveways. No rules either. Just cattails, mud, and murk. Duke and I lived for this. We hunted at Smith's Pond most every day after school, which was only a few blocks away.

Duke had his own agenda – snaring pheasants and rabbits. In this he was defeated daily. I lusted after the beautiful painted pond turtles sunning themselves far out on logs in the murk or giant bullfrogs lurking in the rushes at pond's edge, or the wily and huge water snakes, who could do real damage with their teeth, unlike their smaller relatives in my cellar zoo.

I'd creep up on the snakes and bullfrogs, but no matter how cunning my stealth, they disappeared at the last second in a flash. I constructed a turtle trap, a semisubmersible box with a hole in the top for the turtles to fall into and then be roped to shore. But even the nonchalant turtles were too smart for me.

Duke and I didn't care that we bagged nothing at Smith's Pond. I had enough reptiles and amphibians already. What mattered was the pond itself – about the size of a city block. It was all ours. I never saw another kid or adult there, even though developments encroached on every side and traffic constantly roared from a highway.

Obviously the pond and everything in it were under a death sentence. Only a year after Duke and I left for other hunting grounds at our new house in Bryn Mawr, it was plowed under, burying our marvelous friends without a thought. A half dozen asbestos-sided stick jobs went up with perfect patios, jolly barbecue sets, and TVs with seven channels. The taming of Penn Wynne was complete. An immense boredom settled over the town.

⋘ Every summer when we headed for Ocean City, Duke would hang his head out the car window in the New Jersey Pine Barrens, sniffing the far-off salt air from the bays and marshes. For both of us, a summer of romping was ahead.

At Ocean City, wilderness still had a few years to go. Not far from our cottage, the empty marshlands stretched for miles to the bays, crisscrossed by the gravel roads of speculating developers hoping to pave it all over someday. These roads intersected old drainage ditches that collected runoff which was then coated with oil so that mosquitoes couldn't breed. Mosquitoes were bad for the tourist trade. Of course the oil killed off everything else too. So that scheme was nixed in the forties, and the marshes resurged in time for Duke and me to charge through the tall grasses.

Red-winged blackbirds scolded us; rabbits eluded Duke by the score; diamondback terrapins clomped here and there, too many for my pen.

For the time being, nobody else cared for this desolation. The gravel roads were perfect for Duke's tennis ball retrieves (rocks would do too). Between the rocks, balls, and rabbits, Duke was in a hunter's Valhalla.

At night in his bed next to mine, he'd shiver in dreams of the day's delights.

One afternoon toward the end of summer, our sunset play ended abruptly: ahead on the gravel the body of a dog. At first Duke and I thought it was an old rag rug, then creeping closer, we saw it was indeed a dog, maybe sleeping. But it was for sure dead and all alone and tagless.

Silently we regarded its body. Not a mark on it. No blood. Duke sniffed it, stepped back. He stared at the dog, head down. What was there for us to say? Did the dog have a name? How had he died? Why way out here in the marshes? Hit by a car? No cars here. His death stunned us.

We left him at peace hoping his owners would find him– if he had an owner. We walked home slowly. Duke and I had no answers. Death had not yet figured in our lives.

Ted Kerasote, in *Merle's Door*, describes the moment when his wonderful, and dying, mutt Merle comes upon death beside a Wyoming road– a coyote struck by a car.

> *At the sight of the coyote, Merle had shaken with excitement, but when I had let him out of the car, he had stopped in his rush toward her and raised a paw, expanding and contracting his nostrils like a bellows as he sucked in her scent. In an instant, his excited shivering – "let me at that coyote"– ceased and he became extraordinarily still. With great care, he leaned forward and put*

*his nose a few inches from her belly. Then he eased his nostrils directly into her fur, breathing deeply. Pulling himself back, he looked at me with the sober expression I had seen him wear before.*

*"Dead," I agreed.*

*Gravely, he sat down, cocked his head, and stared at the coyote with the attention that people reserve for unprecedented occurrences. I wondered if this might be the first occasion that he had realized dogs could die . . .*

*I kissed him on the nose, and held his head between my hands, and said, "I will go through this as long as you want." I tried to make my voice reassuring, but his eyes stayed sad and a little frightened and made mine fill with tears.*

*"I will miss you so much," I said, my voice breaking as I tried not to sob in front of him and make him sadder and more fearful for my grief. Swallowing my tears, I added softly, "Love you forever."*

≤§ When Pop was planning to move our family from Penn Wynne to Bryn Mawr, ten miles to the west, I asked him to find a place with lots of woods and a stream for Duke and me.

Pop found just the place in Bryn Mawr, on the border of an old estate, maybe a hundred overgrown acres, the Austin Estate, the last of the Main Line baronial plantations, with a decaying stone mansion in one corner. While our house was going up, I was banging my fort together out of leftover lumber in a backyard mulberry tree.

Swaying in my tree fort, I worshipped God in the clouds, in the sunrises and sunsets, in the stars. The minister's and Pop's prayers often praised the "Glories of Thy

Nature," and I basked in those glories. God was not in cities or suburbs. He was here, speaking to me. I prayed to Him that President Eisenhower and Comrade Khrushchev would not blow up His creation.

Meanwhile there were moral problems to be solved under the fort. That's where you had a deadly contest between good and evil, a contest Duke and I could do something about.

There were good and bad animals. Predators, like foxes and crows, were evil – and those they preyed on, such as rabbits and pheasants, were good. In the junior-high print shop I worked up bold posters that proclaimed "No Hunting" and under that "Predator Hunting Is Ok," and I signed them, "The Henderson Game Commission." Duke was my enforcer, ever on the prowl for whatever moved. The woods behind our house were Austin Estate private property, but I posted the signs on trees for acres.

I myself hunted – righteously, of course. Duke and I hiked through God's woods in search of the devious fox (which we never saw) or the nestling-devouring, egg-sucking crow. Duke chased anything that moved. But he was so clumsy that prey ran right through his legs or shot up under his chin and tumbled him over.

I hunted with a slingshot loaded with unripe wild grapes. The crows hawed at me from the sky as I called to them with my crow-caller and shot hard fruit at them.

But, like gentle Pop, I couldn't abide suffering. He couldn't prune the berserk arms of his fruit trees, and I couldn't make more than feeble passes at crows, post dopey declarations, and build a huge brush pile under my mulberry tree where rabbits, pheasants, and other helpless nobilities could run and hide.

But the greatest of all evils was man's attitude toward the snake. The snake was not slimy, as believed; most were not poisonous; all snakes were terrified of people; they could not roll up in a hoop and attack us; and what's more, snakes were our friends – because snakes ate our enemies, the vermin. It was horrible how people killed snakes for no good reason. So I set out on a one-man campaign to rescue the reputation of the snake. In our eighth-grade public speaking contest, my holy vigor carried me from a classroom appearance to an address before the entire school. I won second prize.

I expected that Duke and my communion with God's Nature would lead to a forestry career, and then I would become United States secretary of agriculture and after that . . .

 

◄§ Dogs were an obsession for our junior high principal, Edward Holyoke Snow. To him life was a dogfight. Snow's favorite slogan, which the entire school – teachers included – was required to chant at pep rallies was, "It's not the size of the dog in the fight, it's the size of the fight in the dog."

Snow prowled the halls, a six-foot, 300-pound, crew-cut, bulldog-jawed fellow in school-colored orange and black socks and tie, his silver whistle swinging from his neck.

The whistle was Snow's gun. By fondling it in a noisy school assembly or by pointing it at a misbehaving kid, he would get instant obedience. And when he actually blew it, followed by his outraged bellow, students shivered and the object of his noise cringed and awaited his judgment. Snow's whistle was no respecter of child, teacher, or God – he'd even blow it in the halls during the morning devotion period, showing a discourtesy to God that I wondered about and then hastily forgot. One didn't question Ed Snow.

Ed Snow rehearsed us in his dog-inspired war games by assembling his troops in the auditorium for any excuse and haranguing us on the evils of pegged pants and DA haircuts; on the glories of Roger Bannister's first mile run in less than four minutes; on obliterating our rival, Upper Darby Junior High School, in every sport.

Snow's Ardmore Junior High School Handbook was my first experience with secular philosophy. It was issued in a new edition each year and included everything I needed to know, from the specific ("All eating is to be done in the cafeteria") to the cosmic: "On the plains of desolation bleach the bones of countless millions who at the moment of victory sat down to rest and resting died." Or mysteriously, "All but the dead left the field."

Real men must win the dogfight of life, and they will if they don't give up. Communism, lying, cowardice, cheating, sneakiness, and sex were bad. He stalked school dances and forbade close dancing.

Snow was quite open about his sex phobia. As a prize for drumming up the most magazine subscriptions for his War Memorial College Scholarship Fund, he bused the top-ten sellers (I was third) to the movie *Battle Cry.*

Unfortunately, he hadn't seen the movie and didn't know that some scenes took place in a whorehouse. I thought they were just friendly ladies. Snow apologized to the school and advised that we boycott the movie.

≈§ Duke was having his own problems with sex – how to get more. Unlike Trixie, he had not been fixed – it was not then the custom – and he was one fully equipped male on the prowl. He would disappear for days seeking dates, once jumping from a second-story window into a snowbank in quest of a neighboring lady. He often didn't return for days. I worried he'd been poisoned, shot, or hit by a car, but he'd always reappear, plastered with burrs and ticks and seeming quite happy with himself.

Me, I was not happy. Getting a girlfriend was far more complicated for me than Duke. For him, great effort paid off. For me there were strange rules to learn. Girls were more complicated than theology.

I looked for help everywhere. Pop's advice, his only sexual advice ever: "Only marry a Christian woman." Mom handed me a pamphlet about venereal disease and said nothing. In those days, nothing was ever said.

I learned about Ben Franklin's virtue chart in a "Personal Growth" leaflet sent to me from the Government Printing Office in Washington, DC. It was one of dozens of leaflets I ordered from a catalog that included titles like "Ten Ways to Become a Winning Public Speaker" or "You and Your Teeth."

I found that many of my virtues were the same ones Ben Franklin was interested in, and, like him, I expected practical results, like a girlfriend, for instance. At Franklin's suggestion, I marked myself every night with pluses and minuses and totaled up the score in the various virtues at the end of each week. I did best in moderation, loyalty, non-boasting, justice, and industry, and not so good in tranquility.

In order to score proper marks in meditation, I had to read at least one "Personal Growth" leaflet and a chapter from the Bible each night, plus enter my ratings on my Virtue Chart. After that, I would turn out the light, open the window wide no matter how cold the weather, and gaze at the stars. I knew God was out there. I would reach out to the sky to touch Him. I expected that one night He would touch me back.

Once Pop opened the bedroom door to say good night, and he saw me reaching to the stars. He didn't say anything, and I didn't either. "Aw, cut that out, Bill," he said finally. I didn't reply.

Pop watched me for a while. I could tell. And then he shut the door.

It was in meditation period that I quite by accident discovered another virtue. I noticed I could produce the most remarkable feelings, actually transport myself into ecstasy, with attention to my crotch. I hadn't imagined that my body could feel as wonderful as this, so transfixed.

It had to be a sin.

Each week I graded myself worse and worse in a category I called "sd" (a meaningless code for what I was trying not to do. I didn't want my biographers to know my shame). I listed this virtue, sd, under the general heading of "Bodily Clean," a class of virtues that included a bath on Monday, Wednesday, and Saturday; clean toenails and fingernails; three full glasses of water a day; and combing my hair.

I became so upset with flunking sd that I flunked myself in the entire Virtue Chart at each week's end. But I couldn't give up the chart, I thought, because I had to grade myself. I didn't trust anybody else's grades – not the church's, not the school's.

Each night I would climb into bed and pray in despair that God would help me stop. And then I asked him to bless Mom and Pop and Bob and Ruth and Trixie and Duke and President Eisenhower.

And then I flunked again.

Duke, with no hands, did far better in this category. He could perform miracles on himself with his tongue that were beyond me.

✎Years before, at Oak Park Fourth Presbyterian Church, Mom and Pop bought me a ten-dollar membership in the I Am His Society. I received an embossed certificate announcing that I had been admitted into a Special Society of the Saved, a society dedicated to lifetime missionary work for Christ. I also got a thin silver ring inscribed with the initials IAH.

I put the ring in my dresser drawer and forgot about it. But in the summer of tenth grade, just after being hired as a boardwalk hot-dog slinger at Mike's Hole in the Wall luncheonette, I found the ring and put it on.

It's not that the ring had some religious significance for me. What it had was something else that I wanted – something solid, to remind me not of Him, but of me. It became the Ring of Myself. When my eyes watered and my voice shook, I would look down at that ring through the tears. I'd see it, and it would remind me never to stop believing in me. To be strong. To buck up. Because I was having trouble remembering who I was. Lots of trouble.

I realized it was impossible for me ever to turn entirely from the church. I would never do such a thing. Of course! In fact, I still walked on the beach at dawn with Duke delivering sermons. "Don't ever forget God!" I yelled at the ocean. "No matter what happens!" I pounded my fist into my palm. Duke cocked his head, worried. He was the only one I could talk to.

Around Labor Day, a girl from school saw me cooking hot dogs at Mike's. She sat down at a stool to ask me how my summer had been.

"I am tearing down truth block by block, and I'll build it up again the same way," I bragged.

"That's nice," she said.

What confidence I didn't get by looking at the Ring of Myself I tried to achieve in high school power games. I applied for and was named drum major of the Lower Merion High School All-Boy Marching Band. In my maroon-and-white drum major's uniform with the gold braid and trim and the three-foot-high fake white rabbit fur hat, I took up my position at the head of the band. With a whistle blast, I announced the start of the half-time football show. That was power. That was Ed Snow. Then I'd shout and do some fancy gestures with my big silver baton. As thousands of Saturday fans watched, I led the band downfield with a determined and flamboyant, duck-footed strut. But the girls were unimpressed.

I was so busy being a powerful person that I worried about neglecting my truth search. With real agony, I wondered, "Would Christ have worn a fake rabbit fur hat?"

◦§ While Duke was roaming the neighborhood in direct pursuit of his sexual goals, I contrived elaborate wooing plans. Then I learned from Will Durant's story of philosophy that Schopenhauer doubted the use of the entire enterprise: "Love is a deception practiced by nature to cover up reproduction." I copied this wisdom into my journal.

But then I read where Emerson said, "To be a Man you must be a nonconformist," so I wrote an essay attacking the shallow beliefs of contemporary Christians and read it aloud in English class.

I expected that lots of girls were going to be impressed

by the new Emersonian me. Except they weren't, not a one.

I did locate one other nonconformist in the eleventh grade, a girl who was rumored to read poetry and paint pictures. So I asked her out. Betty Howard talked nonstop and sneered at school spirit. I sneered at school spirit too and swore that if this date didn't work out, I would give up on girls forever. I took Duke along for moral support.

We drove to Valley Forge, parked under the observation tower, and kissed; she suggested that we climb to the top of the tower, experience Valley Forge and George Washington and the freezing troops in the moonlight, and write a poem.

We climbed over the locked gate with the warning about trespassing and walked the steps to the top. We hadn't started our poem, or even begun to experience the moonlit history yet, when I heard Duke bark a warning. A police cruiser pulled up down below and began poking around my car while Duke snarled at him, putting the cop in a bad mood.

"Up here!" I called helpfully.

The cop picked us out with his spotlight. "We're writing a poem!" I shouted.

When we got down, he wanted to know how old Betty was, figuring on a statutory rape rap. When that didn't work, he wrote a ticket for trespassing on national park property.

Duke let him know what he thought about that.

◄§ A few friends formed the Philosophy Club— about ten of us, boys and girls, eschewing Saturday night dates for the Truth. The existence or nonexistence of God was our topic week after week. Now and then we touched on

Communism and ethics. But what we wanted to settle was "Was He?" or "Wasn't He?"

We scored points on a friend's living-room floor, often not assessing arguments so much as the speaker's lack of intelligence. "You just fell ten points on my list," a class brain informed me after I'd defended God's existence with a quote from the *Reader's Digest*.

Some of them dropped Hegel, Marx, and Wittgenstein into the debate. I doubt if they had actually read the books, but to protect myself against my ignorance of philosophers I hadn't read, I bought a paperback titled *Philosophy Made Simple*. It outlined dozens of thinkers in a few paragraphs each. When confronted, I'd excuse myself to another room, check out *Philosophy Made Simple*, and then rush back with a retort for God's side.

The Philosophy Club argued and argued about the existence of God until we argued ourselves bored. One kid brought a six-pack and told us he'd rather stay high all day than think. We played records and danced.

So I thought up a new club, the Thoreau Club. We'd assemble in a small room at the very top of the high school. The Thoreau Club would be limited to those who really understood the truth. But I never made it very clear to myself or anybody else what it was that they would really understand.

I do remember that around this time I was very fond of the phrase "the soul of nature." Duke was well acquainted with that. He was my apostle to the stars.

◁§ Duke's spirit was guiding me quietly, as we romped through the ruined estate. Without his company I'd have been isolated, endlessly chasing my political, theological, philosophical, and sexual tails.

Nothing should be all this complicated, Duke knew. For instance, Dagger the German shepherd across the street had to be dealt with.

Dagger was younger than Duke and twice the size, about ninety pounds to Duke's forty-five. He belonged to the Youngs, good neighbors. Mr. Young ran a Philadelphia construction company. They had two kids, and Mrs. Young was friends with my mom at church. I never knew who named Dagger or what anger and threat he was supposed to unveil or represent. A dagger he was not. He was actually a sweet fellow who had two major faults: he chased our car and beat up Duke.

The car chasing we tried to correct with explosive devices provided by the Youngs—little firecrackers called Atomic Pearls. My brother and I would lean out the car window and smack the Atomic Pearls onto the asphalt to scare Dagger as we drove up the street. We were quite a noisy family for a few weeks. But Dagger caught on. He ignored the racket and chased us with abandon for the rest of his life, serenaded by Duke's frenzied barking from the backseat.

Duke didn't wallow in mottos and virtue charts to figure out how to deal with Dagger. He didn't need a Ring of Myself. Duke was the frontline defender of his acre at 506 Great Springs Rd., Bryn Mawr, Pennsylvania, and his family. No questions, no qualms. And Dagger was no minor invader. At least once a month, sometimes weekly, he's cross the street and provoke Duke by standing on his land, about a foot from the curb. That did it for Duke. He'd fly across the lawn, yowling threats, and go for Dagger's throat, only to be promptly seized by his own throat and flipped over on his back, pinned by Dagger, who could have broken his neck if he wished.

Duke never stopped struggling and gagging howls. I'd rush out, pull Dagger off, and restrain Duke. Dagger would trot off home, having once more proved he was head capo of the block. Duke was often bloodied and missing a bit of fur, and he was always the loser, the bottom dog. But that didn't stop him the next time Dagger invaded his foot of turf, and the drama repeated itself.

Duke and I roamed Smith's Pond, the Austin Estate, and the Ocean City marshes for the timeless best years of our youth. Later I'd go to college, travel in Europe, and move in with a lady, but he'd always be overjoyed to see me again when I'd return home, even in his feeble last years.

He died in the summer of 1967, when I was in Europe. For a long time his hips were failing, just as Dagger, his arch nemesis, had experienced before dying years earlier. Duke lay in a corner of the yard in a hole of his own making and still he persevered, would not quit. My brother Bob brought him food and water and carried him into the house in bad weather. Finally Duke was too weak to move at all and had to be put down. He was sixteen.

I never got a chance to say good-bye. Bob called me in Berlin to say he was gone.

By then, the developers had carved the Austin Estate into McMansion lots and a fancy retirement home, The Beaumont. Except for occasional lawnmowers or leaf blowers, our fields of joy had gone silent. Ocean City's marshes had long since been paved over. Vacation homes sprouted there. People flocked down from Philadelphia to try to have fun.

⋘ Mary Oliver's poem has always served me as a eulogy
for Duke:

*You do not have to be good.*
*You do not have to walk on your knees*
*For a hundred miles through the desert, repenting.*
*You only have to let the soft animal of your body*
            *love what it loves.*

# Dogless Years

*Dogs are not our whole life, but they
make our lives whole.*

ROGER CARAS

In 1959, I left Duke and our Elysian Fields and trotted
off to college for four years; taught school; lived in Paris,
New York, and elsewhere – and never owned a dog for
twenty years.

They were busy years. Dogs and I met only in passing.

At all-male Hamilton College in upstate New York, a
Gordon setter slunk around the campus – Earl. He
belonged to everybody and nobody. Earl was laughed at,
scared off, seldom petted. He stood apart from the students, a question always in his gaze – would you like me?
Earl was the campus joke.

For a time, Earl and I shared that title. As a freshman,

still infused with Emerson, Thoreau, and glimmers from the Virtue Chart, I petitioned and bullhorned my classmates to resist wearing the obligatory beanie, an ancient and sacred tradition at Hamilton. "Beanies are symbols of degradation, the tattoos of Auschwitz," I preached with a bullhorn from a dormitory window. For my outrage, I was grabbed and flung to the ground after an all-college chapel service and crowned with a baby bonnet. The president of the college, the dean, and eight hundred young men jeered and smiled approval.

I had not been a good little freshman. I still have that baby bonnet.

For the next four years, Earl and I shared a lot in common. We were both outcasts. I returned the favor to the school, utterly bored with its phlegmatic faculty and standardized students. I'd pass by Earl, say hi, and feel his loneliness. But we could do nothing for each other. He wasn't my dog. He was nobody's dog.

I tried to flee the college sophomore year but was stopped by a singular act of affection by my friend Tad, one of 1959's token campus blacks. "I'll miss you," he said simply, perhaps sensing what it was like to be shunned. For that kindness I stayed. Tad and I occupied many of the following years hitchhiking through the Northeast, wherever our thumbs took us, boozing, chasing the ladies.

After graduation I was dogless: at Harvard graduate school (a short stay), teaching sixth grade at a Staten Island prep school, scribbling unpublished short stories, starting my great American novel in a Paris garret– the obligatory year of Parisian starvation for all who would be great American novelists. Back home in Bryn Mawr after my father died, I lived alone, a randy, pathetic bachelor waiting to be drafted and shipped to Vietnam. I drove myself to horrendous daily drunks while a feeble and aging Duke stayed home with Mom.

At a local bar I met an ex-nun who was studying at Bryn Mawr College. She had just divorced Jesus and was no longer Sister Mary Dolores. She married me on the rebound. We needed each other desperately, plus the draft board passed over married men for its ongoing slaughter.

After Bryn Mawr College she studied at Princeton University Graduate School in philosophy, searching in the modern philosophers like Wittgenstein for the Jesus authority she had ditched.

My wife, I discovered, didn't like children or dogs. They made her uncomfortable. Wittgenstein didn't like dogs either. He pooh-poohed any human-dog connection. "If dogs would talk we couldn't understand them," he opined. (The standard retort to that profundity is Wittgenstein can talk and we can't understand him either.)

From Descartes on, philosophy has often denigrated dogs and other animals. The result has been four hundred years of brutalization and laboratory vivisection without benefit of pain relief. Dogs, it seems, don't feel pain, and of course they don't have souls, as the church noted. So dogs have been fodder for our endless cruelty. Here's one of Descartes's disciples, Nicolas de Malebranche, with the master's doctrine on animals:

*There is neither intelligence nor souls as ordinarily meant. They eat without pleasure, cry without pain, grow without knowing it; they desire nothing, fear nothing, know nothing; and if they act in a manner that demonstrates intelligence, it is because God, having made*

*them in order to preserve them, made their bodies in such*
*a way that they mechanically avoid what is capable of*
*destroying them.*

In short, "I think therefore I am, you don't think therefore you aren't."

Any dog owner knows this is a crock. Theologians and
philosophers like Wittgenstein and Descartes, cook up
their crocks, and hope for immortal tenure. Problem is
they never get out of their crock kitchen.

Charles Darwin actually knew an animal or two and
a few dogs also. He noted there is "no fundamental difference between man and the higher mammals in their
mental faculties," pointing out that they experience hap-
piness, wonder, shame, pride, curiosity, jealousy, suspicion, gratitude, and magnanimity, plus love and
sympathy. He said this in 1871. But the Princeton philosophy department didn't consider Darwin a philosopher,
and he never came up at faculty sherries my wife and I
got tipsy at.

We lasted a couple of semesters at Princeton and
headed to Normandy for a year of writing– she a memoir about the convent; me a ghastly novel about a sniper,
since delivered to the landfill.

We ran out of money in Normandy and returned to
New York, where we both worked for commercial book
publishers. The idea of children, or dogs, never came up.
Our lives were as empty as a bare ruined choir. We divorced.

I rented an apartment on Bleecker Street in the Village
– no dogs allowed. Here life got busier– drunken follies,
serial fornications, and the salvation for me: a new publishing company, Pushcart. I jogged on a machine in a
health club watching myself in a huge mirror with

dozens of other joggers, running to nowhere. No dogs allowed. I was far from Duke's bounding fields, half alive and not knowing it. Homeless, and too distracted to see that I had become a cliché, a seventies young man about town.

I joined a group of writers for a winter house rental in Long Island's Bridgehampton and began a memoir about my father I called "my love letter to the world." Mostly I drank at Bobby Van's pub with the other local drinkers with a writing problem. Our mascot was a hefty black Labrador retriever who wandered up and down the icy streets and often joined us in Bobby Van's. "The Mayor of Bridgehampton" Willie Morris christened him. Like Earl, he seemed to belong to everybody and nobody.

❧ My mother, Dorothy Galloway Henderson, honored teacher of high school mathematics, who all her life loved children, dogs, and all the various critters I dragged home, died on September 5, 1980. She left me enough money to buy a summer shack in East Hampton.

This good woman's last dog was a slouching hound named, by me, Snopes, after the aggressive, nasty Faulkner character. My sister, who lived in California, had adopted him to protect mom, who was now alone, visited often by Bob, who lived nearby. Next door was a drug-addicted kid who did time for an armed stickup. He stole from his own parents, siphoned gas from Mom's car, and shot out the windows of Duke's abandoned and decaying doghouse.

Snopes was his equal, the meanest dog ever. No visitor or delivery person was safe from Snopes. As a consequence, he spent most of his last years in the basement waiting for the next-door kid to attack. Upstairs Mom endured experimental breast cancer treatments. She fought on for twelve years before her body let go.

In her last days as she faded in and out of consciousness, I told Mom the most important thing I wanted her to know. "I'm going to get married again and have a child someday!"

I yelled this news into the receiver of a pay phone next to a roaring Long Island highway.

"A baby!" she cried.

"Yes, a baby!" I yelled again, to be sure she remembered what she had heard.

Then I sped to the airport and flew to Bryn Mawr Hospital to be with her for the end. She died surrounded by her three children, at peace, looking forward to her new home in heaven, where I am sure dogs make it through the gates.

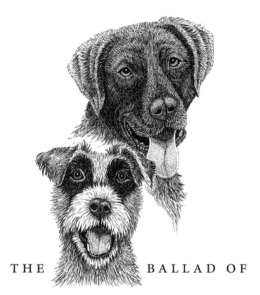

THE BALLAD OF

# Ellen & Rocky

*You think dogs will not be in heaven? I tell you,
they will be there long before any of us.*
ROBERT LOUIS STEVENSON

MILLS HOTEL FOR MEN, NUMBER 2 was engraved in stone over the entrance to the Bleecker Street building in Greenwich Village where I lived. Theodore Dreiser once lived there too, but until a recent remodeling, the Mills Hotel had been a flophouse. I was a thirty-seven-year-old publisher with four titles on my list – the self-published Paris novel I had consumed years in writing, a handbook that told other writers how to publish their own work, and the first two editions of the annual Push-cart Prize anthology of poetry, essays, and short stories from our burgeoning small presses.

Pushcart Press occupied the space under my bache-lor's double bed. The bed filled most of the apartment and was supported by boxes of books. In good weeks, the bed sank closer to the floor as orders left, carried on my back in number one mailbags to the nearby Prince Street post office. In bad weeks, when unsold books were returned, the bed rose again, sometimes at an awkward angle.

I ran my business with an old Olivetti manual type-writer and a PhoneMate answering machine that was losing its voice. I had no money for better machines, and in most months paying the rent was a scramble.

The PhoneMate whispered to me the number of a lady named Annie McCoy who had apparently been search-ing for me since a boozy party weeks before.

I sat at a bar and waited for her. Since the divorce, I trusted no woman and resolved never to trust again. Dat-ing was for laughs. I had developed a tight New York smile.

Finally a woman walked in. Ellen Burstyn, the actress, I thought. I looked at my drink, still unsure, until she walked directly to me and said, "Hi, Bill, I'm Annie. Do you remember me?" she asked, smiling with flawless uptown teeth. From the party I recalled something about her blonde-streaked hair and her fine clothes, which also seemed too very upper East Side.

I quickly downed my wine and ordered another.

"You don't know how hard it was to find you again, Bill. I've been looking all over the whole city. Tell me about yourself."

"I wrote a novel. Nobody wanted it. Had a wife once, too," I blurted. Maybe if I sounded like bad news, Annie would leave quicker.

"Where is the wife now?"

"I really don't know. She shacked up with an ex-con. It's bizarre."

"Why?"

"She's an ex-nun."

I thought this might be too much for Upper-East-Side Annie, a guy married once to an ex-nun. But she didn't blink and kept her eyes on me.

"Did you have any children?"

"No. Kids made her nervous, kids and dogs. I just started a literary anthology," I mentioned. "Published that myself, too, and suddenly the *Times* says I'm an authority. But I'm no authority on anything. In fact, I was fired from every job I ever had. My head spins, my knees wobble from all this notice."

She looked at me without her smile and cocked her head. "Why are your knees weak from notice?" she asked, as if I had a knee disease.

I let it drop. "How about you?" I asked.

"I had a boyfriend until just before I met you at the party. He left me. It's OK, really. I've never been so thrilled. I'm free now! I don't have to report to anybody. I'm a subletter," she said.

We were quiet for a while, thinking of her wonderful new sublet freedom.

We moved to the back room. Over hamburgers and another bottle of wine, Annie sketched her life: daughter of a Mississippi doctor, finishing school, theatrical degree from Northwestern University, early acting rejections in New York, then a side business with a friend – Supergirls, an upbeat outfit that provided any service that was legal. They walked celebrity dogs, babysat exotic birds, scoured the city for rare memorabilia, planned parties, staged publicity stunts, and ended up one night on the Johnny Carson Tonight Show.

But Supergirls was over. Now she was writing a book on contract about the banana business. And she hated bananas.

I told Annie my plans: I would write a memoir about Pop and growing up in a house where we really believed in Jesus, really. Not like the usual equivocating, half-hearted suburban family. "I can't let that kind of faith just slip away and be forgotten. I have to set it on paper, Annie. I'm calling my book *My Love Letter to the World*."

Home suddenly seemed wonderful to me, a steady, kind vision in a boozy, hectic universe. Home, how far away. Trixie, Duke, Boots the cat?

Annie and I were awash in wine, hamburgers, and autobiography. "I'll show you my publishing office," I offered.

Holding hands, we headed out into the cold Village night.

By dawn, most of the wine's effects had left me. I remember a bright sunrise and Annie's golden hair, formerly the dyed hair of an Upper-East-Side type, now the glory of a caring lady who had traveled downtown to my hovel in the Mills Hotel for Men.

That morning we searched for a permanent place for Annie. Some new apartments were going up around the corner. Since Annie had an ancient Persian cat named Sebastian, she needed a pet-friendly place. Together we explored the empty rooms.

At lunch she told me about a puppy she had rescued from under the wheels of traffic on Broadway a few weeks back. She and a friend had been to see the musical

*Mame.* They had gone to dinner at Sardi's and were strolling up Broadway when a small "thing" scurried across the still busy street and hid under a parked car. Annie was sure it was a dog and patiently lured it out – a puppy, scared, lost, and very glad to be swept up into her arms and carried home. Annie had thought about keeping him, but she was living out of a suitcase. She ran an ad, a man called – was the dog by any chance a beagle? The man said he had three grieving children at home. Their beagle had just been run over. Annie seemed sure there was probably beagle in him. By the time the man, now identified as a policeman, arrived with his wife, the pup, nicknamed Broadway, was busy chewing up a shoe and peeing at will. The policeman and his wife took one look. He was no beagle but "close enough," said the grateful cop. "We can't go home empty handed."

Annie, it turned out, adored dogs.

ᐱᔥ On a Sunday night months later, Annie and I went to a quietly boring movie in midtown. Afterward, quietly bored, I said good night to Annie, who was preserving her independence that night by sleeping uptown in her own bed by herself.

I walked south toward the Forty-Second Street subway stop at the Port Authority Bus Terminal. A calm night, lots of people about.

Suddenly they were on both sides of me, two of them, one at each elbow. "Cocaine, cocaine? Want cocaine, mister?" They grabbed my elbows and propelled me down the street into the light of a restaurant window.

One spun me out to face the street, locked my neck in a choke hold, and slammed my head against the window behind him. He ripped out my wallet and discovered seven dollars.

People gathered to stare.

"No good! No good!" He waved the money in my face. "Very bad. We got to do something about this." But before he could "do something," he and his pal were surrounded by six cops, four in plain clothes, all with guns pointed.

In two minutes it was over.

One cop showed me a knife with a foot-long blade that had been hidden in the choker's boot and probably meant for my throat a few seconds later.

Attempting again a strong, youthful stride, I made it back to Bleecker Street. But I knew my youth and my stride wouldn't protect me in this city anymore. Perhaps I had always walked like an easy mark, a friendly guy who wouldn't struggle, the kind of guy who felt sorry for his muggers, so stupid that they attacked on a crowded, cop-ridden street. They were stupid or crazy.

Six blocks north of this spot at noon, a mugger had slashed a woman's throat when she refused to release her handbag. She died on the sidewalk in the mess of her own blood, while people on their lunch hours gawked.

Stupid or crazy. It made no difference now.

It was time to move. I wanted Annie to go with me.

New York cramped me with horror, with crowds. Long ago I had resolved never to get near New York. It was the center of middlemen, hustlers, compromisers, and worst of the lot, publishers. Publishers, I declared, traded with words and corrupted truth for profit. Back then I wanted nothing to do with them.

For Annie, too, it was finished.

As a girl in Holly Springs, Mississippi, Annie had envisioned New York as the city of glamour and excitement just like in the movies, but her acting career never happened, and soon Supergirls faded from that Johnny Carson high.

People constantly stopped her on the street and asked for her autograph. She was tired of explaining that she was not Ellen Burstyn. She signed Burstyn's name on anything just to escape.

How could she tell them she was only the would-be author of a book about bananas?

Annie came to New York to dream. Now others dreamed her as somebody else. I came to New York as a compromise.

For both of us it was over.

We planned to escape to that summer shack in East Hampton. We could bicycle to the post office, bicycle to the market, bicycle to the beach, bicycle to somewhere real without the health club mirror. And maybe get a dog. It had been two empty decades without Trixie or Duke in my life.

Annie and I didn't call it marriage. We didn't call it anything.

In May 1981, we packed our few things into a small U-Haul truck and headed east down the Long Island Expressway.

Waiting for us was a dinky summer place with bunk beds in two small, dark bedrooms and a huge bamboo tiki bar that took up most of the kitchen. Annie was doubtful, but it was all I could afford with my mother's gift. The land around it was as spectacular as the house was ordinary. The beach was a short walk down a dirt road, and on days with a northwest wind, the surf roared onto the sand, and the harbor bell buoy clanged.

As we drove that last mile to the house, leaving New York forever, we passed under a bower of just-blooming dogwood blossoms. The pink and white blossoms formed a flowered path for our arrival.

I parked the U-Haul on the sandy driveway, and we began carrying out enough gear to last our first night. Annie stuck a bottle of champagne in the refrigerator for a toast.

I was standing at the back of the truck in the twilight when I saw a figure stalking through the dogwoods toward me. He had no reason to be there, but this was the crime-free sticks, and I wasn't concerned. Probably a neighbor dropping by to say welcome.

With him were two German shepherds, yanking at their leashes. When they spotted me, they began to howl. Sweet Dagger dogs these were not. Under his arm he cradled a shotgun.

He halted a few feet away, barely keeping the dogs from me.

"What do you think you're doing?" he demanded.

Annie came out of the house. "What's in the truck?" he asked her.

She told him it was our furniture, and we had just arrived from the city. We would live here.

"We have a rapist on the loose. He just attacked a lady at the beach."

With that he headed back into the night. I never learned if he was a cop or just a civilian on posse patrol.

Quietly, we drank champagne.

That night we left the outside spotlight on and slept

very little. This was not starting out well. To create a home, perhaps to save our lives, we resolved to get a dog.

❧ The next day we went looking for a dog. We checked out the *East Hampton Star* and various postings at the general store and found nothing.

Days later, driving aimlessly about, we passed a sign: Free Chesapeake Bay Retriever Pups. Ready Now.

"Want to see?"

"OK," said Annie.

I had heard of "Chessies" – a vague image in my mind of a noble dog jumping into the icy water after ducks. And these Chessies were free!

The owner explained that all the puppies had been adopted except for one, and she was in the garage. There were no papers. I silently questioned if these were really Chessies. Often local Labrador retrievers were advertised as "Labs" if they had just a tinge of Lab in them and looked Labbish. Maybe this Chessie was a mutt in fake plumage.

The young, dark brown dog with a white front and floppy ears had probably been in that garage for a long time. She was no puppy. She was delirious to see us, wiggles and leaps and yowls of greeting.

"She's a bundle," explained the owner. "Last of the litter."

I thought to ask why she had been rejected by other adopters but didn't. Neither Annie nor I could resist this onslaught of yearning.

"She's been spayed too. So you don't have to worry about that," said the owner. "She'll need some room to exercise, though," he observed. "Lots of energy."

I could see that. The dog was pirouetting for us.

"Please, please, please," she sang. "Get me out of this garage."

Nothing to squabble about here. The dog made up our minds. The owner found a leash and collar, and off we went with our new child.

"Do you think we should have looked around more?" asked Annie as the dog bounced around the car.

"Too late now," I said.

Our new life had begun.

We took the freed dog directly to the beach and let her tear about. She ran like she had never before seen sand, sea, or sky. Maybe she hadn't.

I left Annie and the Chessie there and went for dog chow with a side visit to the library to belatedly investigate what we had just done. I consulted a dog encyclopedia under "Chesapeake Bay Retriever, Chessies, Chessie Dog." I learned that the breed supposedly originated in 1804 when a ship from England wrecked on the Maryland coast. Everybody made it to shore, including two Newfoundland dogs, who promptly mated with local retrievers, and a new breed was born.

Chessies need dominant humans, the book said, or they tend to take over: "They are strong and require a strong master." If they lack exercise, they behave badly. But otherwise they are friendly, intelligent, obedient, courageous, willing, loving, good with kids and cats, but a bit slow to learn. They have a dense, waterproof coat and prefer to sleep outside. They are almost unstoppable as retrievers, with webbed feet for a fast paddle and boundless drive. In fact, one Chessie was said to have retrieved two hundred ducks in a single day's hunt.

Back at the beach I found Annie sitting on a dune,

alone. Far in the distance a dark spot, our Chessie, tore circles on the sand and then jetted back to us and off again in the other direction. When the sun got to her, she plunged into the water, cooled off, and charged out, ready for another marathon of nonstop frolic.

We finally caught her at dusk and drove back to our shack, where she collapsed into an exhausted sleep on the floor, ignoring the soft rug Annie had put down for her.

At dinner we discussed our explosive new friend. What to call her? We filtered through dogs' names from long ago: Popeye was Annie's first dog so maybe Olive Oil? I suggested Tyde (who lived in Buster Brown's shoe on my favorite Saturday morning 1940s radio program) or Queen, after Sergeant Preston of the Yukon's dog, King.

"Lassie?" I joked.

" 'Loopy' is more like it."

"Zip."

"Zoom."

"Zany."

Nothing fit.

"How about your arch nemesis. The person you can't get rid of, who rules your life?"

"Who? You?"

"Ellen Burstyn."

So Ellen Burstyn it was.

And indeed Ellen did just that – ruled our lives through all that late summer, fall, and winter – a hand-chewing (no licks or cuddles), skinny, unfenceable, uncontrollable riot of flipped-out energy. She was totally useless as a guard dog, since she had no sense of territory. All the neighborhood, empty now of summer renters, was hers, and she streaked here and there with abandon. Attempts to calm her or even to keep her inside were futile. She jumped out windows and over furniture (never around) and chewed up most of it. She leaped onto counters and tables to devour what she wished and did not fear my reprimands. I attempted a strong command voice – as the dog book had suggested – but she ignored me. It wasn't that I was meek and she in charge; it was merely that she didn't recognize me at all.

Annie and I ran her daily on the beach, but she exhausted both of us. Even the ancient Labrador retrievers next door, Nugget and Sally, wanted nothing to do with her as she nipped and yapped at them, "Play! Play! *Carpe diem!*" They snarled and took a snooze.

Elizabeth Marshall Thomas in her recent *The Social Life of Dogs* advises, "I don't give my dogs much training because I want them to do their own thinking, to do what they want rather than wait to see what I want. If I train them, they learn from me. If I don't train them, I learn from them."

With almost all the dogs I have owned, I agree with this advice. I prefer to negotiate than to spew out orders. To hit or yell is to me a misbehavior on my part.

Thomas says she teaches only five things: the meaning of no; to come when called; to urinate and defecate outdoors only; not to take human food; never to chase a car but to sit while it goes by.

Ellen ignored all of these, except the outdoor bathroom tip. She was pretty good with that.

When it was duck hunting season, guns roared every dawn in the harbors. I thought of hiring Ellen out or hunting duck myself. But sitting in a cold brush blind of a gray morning wasn't the least enticing even in daydreams, and I knew Ellen, who desperately needed something to do, wasn't suited for retrieving or any occupation. She was indeed a party girl in constant, fruitless search for a party.

She needed a friend to party with. We headed off to East Hampton's Animal Rescue Fund to find her such a friend.

ARF (Animal Rescue Fund) is the Hamptons' idea of a dog pound. Every dog is cared for as part of the ARF family including daily walks with volunteers, and personal interviews and walks with prospective adopters (who are thoroughly screened). In a typical year, hundreds of dogs are saved from puppy mills, natural disasters, the mean streets, or homes where they are no longer welcome. ARF is a nonprofit volunteer organization and a model to the rest of the country for a no-kill shelter. Friendly dogs take long recesses with pals in outside enclosures. Snooty or mean dogs sit by themselves, as they seemed to prefer. No dog or cat is ever destroyed. They have lifetime tenure at ARF.

This club atmosphere, however, didn't reduce the poignancy of our visit. Each dog longed for a home. So did Annie and I. The howls and cries and frantic ripping at cages and fences tore at us.

One little dog– Rocky was the tag on his enclosure– didn't cry out. He sat looking at us with asking eyes. Didn't say a word. We sensed a dignity, a politeness.

"May we walk him?" we asked.

"The Norman Rockwell dog? Sure," replied the volunteer.

She was right. Rocky was the Everyman mutt, right out of a Rockwell painting. He was about three years old, short, a bit stocky, lop-eared, brown, about fifty pounds, with dark raccoon circles around his eyes. Rocky Raccoon!

On our get-acquainted stroll we met a world-class mutt, calm, obedient, mannerly, and friendly, but not a gusher of licks and scrambles. Somehow Annie and I had stumbled on to the perfect partner for Ellen. He was everything that Ellen was not. If it's true that in marriage opposites attract, these two were wed in heaven. Ellen adored Rocky and he admired her. They became a neighborhood social pair, visiting the few year-rounders regularly as if invited. There was no harm in them, only greeting. And they were welcomed in turn and fed snacks, petted. They made a remarkable pair – the wild lady and her gentleman escort.

Annie and I could have learned from their example – there was trouble brewing in our beach shack. Annie, daughter of Southern gentry, was used to better housing, and after a year of patching up and making do, she had had it.

To me, a house was something to keep the rain off and the cold out. The dwelling was not important as long as you lived a worthy life inside it. A house was useful only in keeping the writers and publishers of words warm and the paper dry.

A house might have other minor uses, too: as an investment, for instance – the only investment I would ever make, thanks to my mother's dying gift. But otherwise, a house meant bills for improvements, repairs, and taxes.

To Annie, a house was a place for fine old furniture handed down from generation to generation. A house was a reflection of who you were. A house was at least half of us, and this half was a shanty.

"I want another house," she complained.

But there was nothing I could do for Annie. I would not sell my first and perhaps only property. Annie, half-heartedly, thought about buying her own house with her father's help. She invited me to rent out the shanty and join her, but I said no.

Things were getting shaky between us.

Still, Annie cooked with ceremony. No dinner was ever thrown on the table. She devoted entire afternoons readying her daily menus. Annie's seafood pasta, Annie's crab cakes, Annie's own shepherd pie, Annie's stuffed game hen, Annie's Moroccan tagine.

But it was clear she was conflicted. It was increasingly confusing to me but even more so to her. With her old acting skills kicking in, the lament over our life together grew into rambling soliloquies. "In one day I can love you and hate you," Annie would begin over another extraordinary meal. Sometimes she "was leaving," or she might stay but only if I changed, or she missed the excitement of New York; any one of a number of ills was ascribed to me, to our life, to this "loathsome place."

Loathsome was one of Annie's favorite words. She strung out the "loo."

Stilled by the food and wine, I had no reply. I nodded and drank. After all, we weren't married. This was all an experiment, increasingly a failed experiment?

Not so for our dogs. Ellen's chaos, a reflection of our own, was over. Sweet Rocky became her solace. That winter even as Annie and I battled over life together, we sang the ballad of Ellen and Rocky.

Since Ellen preferred to sleep outside, Rocky spent most nights with her on the patio chaise lounge. In the distance they could see the moon shining off the bay and hear the calling of gulls and the clang of the harbor bell buoy. When it rained or snowed, Ellen deigned to sleep inside on the couch, and Rocky followed her.

I decided they needed a doghouse. With only a tree fort to my construction credit, I winged it as best as I could. Rocky and Ellen's doghouse was banged together out of two-by-fours and cedar shingles, about three feet high and wide enough for both of them. I placed two doors next to each other, Rocky painted over one and Ellen over the other. Ellen promptly took over both doors and blocked Rocky out.

We let them run loose, since there were no town leash laws and, in winter, few cars. Our only concern was a grumpy "German" who lived in an ugly brick house around the corner and who played loud polka music on his stereo. He was rumored to hate dogs– they might poop on his little lawn.

(If he was so poop-obsessed, he might have read J. R. Ackerley's exquisite and hilarious *My Dog Tulip*, first published in 1956. It is the definitive dog memoir on poop and doggy sex, handled with grace and wit.)

Often Annie and I had to visit New York on business, to see old friends. The city had lost all attraction to me, and I'd rush back on the train the same day, anxious to return to our family. Always the dogs were there to welcome me with Ellen's wiggles and Rocky's grin.

On April 4, 1982, Annie was visiting with her family, and I had spent a rare night in the city. When I drove up to the house, the dogs were gone. Perhaps I thought they were investigating the beach or making the rounds of the neighbors. I waited. I searched the beach, circled the neighborhood on my bike, calling out. Silence.

When they didn't return that night, as they had always

done, I began to feel the creep of horror. I knocked on doors. Nobody had seen them. But where could they have gone?

I was sure they'd been kidnapped. Perhaps a biological lab had snatched them, and they were caged, awaiting ghastly experiments. I drove around town, suspicious of every truck and van, peering in the windows, on the verge of challenging drivers. "What have you done with our dogs?" I also kept an eye on the German's place.

Annie returned from her trip, and we worried together with rising panic.

We advertised in the classified section of the local paper. "Dogs missing . . ." We posted the village and the woods with signs offering a fifty-dollar reward for information or sightings of the dogs. Kids called, hoping for the fifty dollars. "I saw a black dog around here yesterday . . ." But it was never Ellen or Rocky.

We searched the state park nearby and asked the ranger if he had seen a small mutt with raccoon eyes or a retriever. He hadn't, but we noticed newborn white Labrador puppies penned outside his office. They were round, and they were tripping over themselves to say hello, and they were for sale.

Annie and I borrowed a bullhorn and drove through the woods. "Rocky, Ellen. We're here . . ." Annie called out of the car window. Nothing. Not a shred of response. Her words traveled through the brown, empty woods and didn't stir the dogs where they floated in the new, unfenced pool of a developer's all-white, high-tech spec house.

A real estate agent found the dogs. She was showing the spec house to clients and discovered Rocky and Ellen drifting. She telephoned the dog warden, and he told me where they were, just a half-mile from our house. A badly secured tarpaulin covering the pool had given way beneath them.

"What do you want to do about it?" asked the dog warden.

"Do?"

"The bodies."

"What can I do?"

"Up to you. I can take them to the dump."

"Yes."

"That's it?"

"Yes."

I was struck stupid with shock. Dead in a pool? The developers had been marching like vandals across East Hampton's woods– knocking up huge fake, cheap modern boxes in (correct) speculation that someday somebody would pay a fortune for them.

And now they had taken our dogs.

When I snapped out of it, I rushed to the spec house before the dog warden could get to them. It was a perfect spring day, dazzlingly bright with a hint of green and red in the budding trees. The sun glared off the pool into my eyes as I pushed open the unlatched gate and saw them floating in the cold water, Rocky at one end, Ellen at the other, each close to the pool wall where they had drowned. All around the wooden trim were the claw marks they had left as they tried to get a grip and climb out.

How long had they struggled? Did they hear me calling from my bicycle that day I returned from the city? Had I missed their barks? I wasn't far off. Did they really die from drowning or from the near-freezing water? It had been a very cold spring.

They lay tangled in the poorly attached cover. The pool ladders were not yet installed, a slapdash, slob's job, in a hurry for a profit. There was no way out for them, except me, and I had not heard them.

I knelt down and lifted them out, icy, stiff. I laid their bodies on the deck and just stared at what had so joyously been and now was so stupidly gone. Then I put them in the car's trunk and drove home to Annie.

Years later, Annie and I – and our eight-year-old daughter, Holly– sailed to England on the *Queen Elizabeth 2*. The voyage was my birthday present to Annie, her fiftieth. I maxed out my credit card for the grand occasion.

Annie was writing a novel about Margaret Bourke-White, the photographer, who had once gone down with a ship during WWII and was lost at sea. We were invited to the captain's chambers to learn more about sea catastrophes. (Holly was allowed to hold the ship's wheel and steer the *QE2*.) The captain's second in command, who had once been a common seaman, almost drowned off the Falkland Islands when the Argentine navy sank her majesty's frigate in the Falkland War. He swam as long as he was able in the forty-degree water.

"What was it like?" I asked.

"You get tired, very tired, the cold numbs everything. After a while you just give up. It's kind of peaceful."

He was saved with minutes left.

I hoped it had been that way for Rocky and Ellen at the end, after all the clawing and calling. Peace.

Recently a friend told me of his near drowning at a Southampton beach. He was seven; the tide took him out. "At first you struggle like hell. Then you give up. I'm not kidding, cliché or not, your whole life flashes before you in an instant, all of my seven years. Then you stop struggling and a kind of peace comes over you, and a bright light."

He too had been hauled out at the last instant.

I pray this is what it was like for Ellen and Rocky as we called to each other through the woods. I hope at the last that Rocky dreamed of Ellen and their brief romance, and Ellen dreamed of the little neutered gent, her first and only boyfriend, before they both went under.

✒ After Annie and I dug a grave for them near a leaning, hurricane-blasted oak in the backyard; after we laid them on soft towels with their toys and milk bones for the next life; after we filled in the hole and posted a notice on the tree about just who was buried there, we both cried out of control.

After my crying was done, I went berserk with rage.

I would burn down the speculator's house. Such people had stolen Smith's Pond, the Ocean City marshes, and the Austin Estate from Duke and me, and now this guy had actually murdered my friends with an illegally unfenced pool. I would go there at night, splash the high-tech joint with gasoline, and off it goes. I didn't tell Annie what I planned.

But the next day, before my arson, I telephoned the builder. Very quietly – too quietly – I explained what he had done to us. I expected him to make restitution – a hundred-dollar check made out to ARF and in my hands in twenty-four hours. I hung up. His lawyer called back:

"He's fully protected by insurance," complained the lawyer. Still oddly quiet, I said, "I don't care about that," and hung up.

He cut the check. I didn't burn his house.

The *East Hampton Star* honored Rocky and Ellen with an obituary of sorts: "Dogs Die in Pool," announced the headline, noting that by law pools had to be fenced and securely covered, otherwise children might drown.

My rage subsided and went underground. But the tears hit anytime.

For Annie it was far worse. Her father had died in her arms less than a month before. At seventy-two years old, he had just returned home after trying to lose weight quickly at a clinic.

Annie had held him. As a doctor, he knew what was happening. A massive internal hemorrhage. But he didn't want her to call for help. "Sit me on the couch," he said. "You stay here and don't leave me."

He was very clear.

Annie did as she was told.

She watched him turn bone white, heard his death rattle. She ran to get her sleeping mother in the next room. He looked at both of them brightly and died.

Annie had not been able to cry then, nor at his funeral.

When Ellen and Rocky died, she sobbed for the dogs and for her daddy and would not get out of bed.

Ellen and Rocky had taught us how two very different personalities can love each other. In the months ahead we were in danger of losing that lesson. Somehow it had to be restored before chaos overtook us.

From the vantage point from which I write, it is hard to believe how closely Annie and I came to mucking up our lives. However, we were about to embark on just such a course. It would be one hell of a confusing and bumpy road for the next year. At the end of the road there would be a tiny and perfect baby. At the beginning there was a tiny and perfect dog.

# Sophie

*My little dog – a heartbeat at my feet.*
EDITH WHARTON

I DIDN'T KNOW what to do for Annie. She seemed beyond consolation – utterly destroyed. Then I remembered the puppies in the park. I told her I was going to have a look at them. She refused to let me take my wallet – if I bought a dog, we might have to go through all this dying again, she cried.

I handed her my wallet but slipped a check in my back pocket.

There they were in their chicken-wire pen, all eight of them, just as Annie and I had stumbled upon them while searching for Ellen and Rocky. Yellow Labrador retrievers, almost white, they fell over themselves in eagerness, but one seemed more eager than the others. I picked her up, a ball of hot energy.

"Fifty dollars," said the park ranger who lived on the premises. "No papers. Mom and pop are around here somewhere. Real Labs."

The mother and father were nowhere to be seen. But it all seemed honest enough.

"That's fine with me." I wrote him a check and carried my atomic bundle to the car.

When Annie looked up from her bed, the puppy sat in my palm, all tongue and exclamations. Annie took her in her arms and laughed.

We named her Sophie, because she was as soft and overstuffed as a sofa. Her newborn joy made our sorrow seem like bad form. Sophie slept on our bed. She swam in the sound, lost her puppy fat, and grew large and strong. For a while her spirit was contagious. Annie and I recovered from the Rocky and Ellen disaster and hoped all of this might work out. Our passionate puppy kept us from slipping apart.

The veterinarian told us that many people spayed their females after six months. Otherwise, they would go into heat and howl and tear up the rug and draw males who would sit outside waiting, snarling, and crapping. Most people thought that situation was inconvenient, he said.

One cold October morning, I walked into the bedroom where Sophie slept on her spot on the bed and fastened a leash to her neck. She thumped her tail and licked my hand, thinking a walk was coming up.

I was hung over, grumpy, and loose of tongue from yet another of the dinner parties that we and our friends gave for each other in constant rounds. We were all childless couples. A new country emptiness had replaced the free fucking nothingness of the city. I saw myself slumping into middle age, publishing one book after another, creeping to the end. A spirit was leaving my noncommercial cathedral.

And Annie too was growing anxious. Our shack was still a shack, and we were going nowhere.

That morning, I snapped Sophie's leash on her collar. "Come on, Sophie. Let's get sterile, like everybody else," I snarled. "Sterile is in this year."

Annie and I looked at each other, startled at what my hangover had just revealed.

That night, while Sophie recuperated from her operation at the animal hospital, I dreamed I was holding my just-born child in my arms. A great white light shone around my child and me. I said in my dream, "This is what it is all for."

In ecstasy, I woke up.

Annie woke at the same moment. "I was just dreaming," she said. "Maybe we could adopt a baby."

It seemed the only way. Annie was past forty by now. And she lacked an ovary, removed years ago in an operation for a benign cyst. Dream mates, we hugged each other and slept.

Sophie's spaying had started us out on a long sojourn.

❧ In New York, Annie had lunch with Timmie, an ex-Supergirl who had just had a baby boy at thirty-nine. Timmie brought the baby along, and he slept in a basket on the table between them.

Annie told Timmie about her great fall from New York to a shack, about living in holy literary poverty, about adopting a child, or even having one of our own, but it was probably too late . . .

"Do it!" Timmie interrupted and banged her hand on the table.

The baby woke up.

"I'm too old. I've got one ovary left. There are too many tests," Annie said.

"Do it! Get the tests. Do everything! You haven't got a whole lot of time!"

The baby started to cry. Timmie lifted him from the basket and handed him to Annie. He calmed down, stopped crying.

"Children are the only thing in the world," Timmie told Annie. "The only thing."

ク Dr. Carol Livoti, the baby doctor recommended in New York, called to confirm the appointment Annie had made from a pay phone after her lunch with Timmie. Dr. Livoti was an Italian mama gone undercover as a practitioner of medicine.

"And don't worry about that one-ovary stuff. You can have a baby with half an ovary," Carol proclaimed.

At her office, Dr. Livoti did a basic exam and pronounced Annie fit. She handed Annie a plastic cup. "We test him first. The sperm goes in this cup and the cup goes to this laboratory." She scribbled the New York address of the lab, hand delivery required.

In East Hampton, Annie looked after Sophie. We had to confine her in the house after her spaying. She wanted to bounce around the neighborhood, but in her first foray, the polka-blasting German fellow had apparently hit her with his car, not badly, but enough to bust two of her stitches and send her back to the vet. "I hit your dog! Keep that stinking mutt off my property!" our polka friend hollered into our phone. He'd meant to remain anonymous but forgot to turn down the music in the background.

No way would we, or could we, keep Sophie tied up. She would have her freedom soon, and now, thanks to the German, she knew to be wary of cars.

Carol Livoti's review was upbeat. "You next, Annie."

Annie reported to Livoti's New York office for her first test, a biopsy of the remaining ovary, a particularly nasty and embarrassing procedure, performed while she was spread on a table under bright lights. Dr. Livoti called the next day to announce that she had passed the test. The second test, a fallopian tube blowout, was set for seven days later.

The day before the blowout, Annie and I talked it all over at a local diner. "I only have one tube, so maybe it won't be too bad," she said optimistically.

As our sandwiches arrived, Annie suddenly said, "Are you intending to become a born again?"

I shook my head and smiled. I had watched Jimmy Swaggart, the evangelist, on TV the evening before, fascinated by his talent and moved against my will. "He's a great religious actor. That's all."

"Because I don't want a religious nut as father to my child. All of this is moving too fast. I'm so unhappy. I don't know where to go or how to start going there."

That night, before the next test, the weather report warned of near-blizzard conditions for the next day. It would probably be impossible to get to New York anyway. Annie and I decided to let the weather decide for us.

The next day was frigid with a hazy sunrise. Annie caught the first train to New York. She and Carol watched on the screen as the dye flowed painlessly through the clear tube. Dr. Livoti was pleased. "There's nothing wrong with you."

Afterward, Annie visited a woman psychologist and asked for advice. The psychologist told Annie she could do anything she wanted to do. All Annie had to do was make up her mind what it was she wanted to do.

As she was riding back to East Hampton, the blizzard struck from the northeast with classic force. Ten inches of snow collected in an hour. By mid-Island, she could see nothing outside the window.

It was so bad by the time Sophie and I arrived at the train station to meet her that the ticket agent told me the Long Island Rail Road system was near collapse. Switches were frozen, signal lights out. The drifts piled halfway up the station wall. Annie's train was three hours late when I heard the whistle from the west and then saw the train's headlights dimly through the whiteout.

The train stopped. Forms struggled off. I couldn't find her. "Annie!" I yelled into the snow. "Over here! I'm down this way!" Sophie barked directions.

Then from the other side of the station, I heard her calling. "Bill, Sophie, where are you?"

🥬 For the anniversary dinner of our first meeting, Annie had cooked a lamb stew. I opened a special bottle of Médoc and waited at the dining room table, forbidden to help her, as always, in her careful preparation.

I had just salvaged the table from the town dump, and I was proud of it. The dump was a treasure trove of discarded items from upscale estates. The rich did not stage yard sales for chump change. Sofas, vintage chairs and tables, lawn furniture with perhaps a small stain or scratch were hastily removed to the dump's home exchange area. Most of our furniture was rescued from the dump.

"We have to talk," she announced.

"About what?" I smiled.

"Us."

"OK."

"I am going away to think. This is moving too fast."

"Really?" I was bewildered. And helpless.

"Yes. Really!"

I sat in the chair while she banged around in the tiny bedroom, packing her things into two suitcases. She threw her bags into the front seat of the car. I touched her arm. "Where are you going?"

"That shrink said I'd have to make up my mind, and I have. I am going!"

"Please do me one last favor? Wait until morning. You can't drive around out there in the dark with no place to go."

I took the car keys from her hand. "You can leave in the morning. I'll help you find a place to stay."

She ran into the bedroom.

I lay on the couch, sleepless. Sophie lay on the floor between us.

On the couch I watched the sky brighten over the sound. The birds were in full racket. A deer poked around the front yard.

Annie woke and headed into the kitchen. She cooked grits, once-over-lightly eggs, and Canadian bacon. Without a word, she put it on the table in front of me. "I decided not to go," she said.

"I think you should go, Annie. You have always wanted to leave. Your bags are packed. Go. Do it now. Figure it all out."

I was seeing it her way, I thought. She was exactly who she envisioned she was – a woman of enormous talent, imagination, and charm. But I was not worth the pain I gave her in return. Plus, after her parents' sad example, motherhood and marriage could only seem like slow death.

There had to be a better place for Annie than this shed. She ought to be swept away in romance. All she got from me was furniture from the dump and my head-scratching bewilderment. A guy who thought money was germs. She was on the wrong side of the highway.

At ten o'clock, she left, sobbing.

Sophie stared after her.


Without Sophie's company I would have fled the emptiness of the beach shack. There was another good woman who, during our months of turmoil, I had met in New York at a publishing party and who was interested in love, children, and a white picket fence cottage. I could have gone to her. Instead I stayed put with Sophie.

Sophie was a great teacher – nothing kept her down. She was literally unsinkable. On the beach she dove for rocks and swam out for sticks. The sticks were almost too easy for her, a toss, a splash, a paddle: "Here's your stick back, Bill." The rocks were more interesting. I'd sail them out twenty feet or more, and she'd dive to the bottom, root through other stones down there, and return with the precise rock I'd thrown.

That spring the sun was always out, it seemed, illuminating the white dog and me. What a fine mother Sophie would have been, I pondered, what a ferocious, loving mom to her kids. And we had ended it all with her spaying– the sterile couple syndrome. Not that Sophie realized what she was missing. But I felt guilty at my timidity. Why shouldn't she have remained fertile? So what if horny males parked on our driveway when she was in heat, howling and banging on the door. In New York, I'd been such a male myself. Perhaps some ex-girlfriends thought I'd have been better off neutered too.

Unlike Ellen, unsinkable Sophie was focused on her passions. If she pursued a tennis ball, she belonged to that ball, body and soul. If she hiked with me through the woods or along the beach, she was my constant companion and never drifted off after an interesting sniff or fascinating scuffle. And at night she always slept at the foot of our bed waiting for Annie to return.

Sophie was excessively loyal. She refused to let other dogs approach me, even the most friendly. Lapdogs and mastiffs were run off. Unlike Duke, who defended only his one acre of suburbia from the teasing Dagger, Sophie protected everywhere we went as her inviolable turf. Once, while chasing stones on the shore, she spotted a Yorkie snoozing under an old man's beach chair. Before I could stop her, she raced over, dragged the Yorkie out, and shook it, knocking the man to the sand and leaving me to grovel in apologies.

Dogs trotting by the car on the road were not spared Sophie's territorial wrath and received a good barking. Once she shoved open the tailgate and hit the pavement at thirty-five miles an hour, rolling and howling at a passing mutt who was amazed at this suicidal nut. I thought she was dead, but back into the car she leaped.

Sophie loved human beings. Among her few faults was an extreme gregariousness. Like Will Rogers, she never met a person she didn't adore. Everybody got a kiss from Sophie. At cocktail parties she'd circle the room, greeting all the guests and smashing glasses and dips to the floor with her whirlpool tail.

Our portion of East Hampton wasn't big enough for Sophie. Because she seemed well aware of the danger of cars– thanks to the assault of the German polka fanatic– and because the town had no leash law, and she was unchainable in any case, I let her explore at will. Always, by some method, she'd find her way home by night, often via my chauffeur service. A phone call: "These tags say you own a Labrador retriever named Sophie. She's here." And off I'd go, sometimes quite a distance, to find Sophie in the twilight, happily awaiting me on the porch of her new friends.

Her grand adventure was a five-mile trot into the center of East Hampton village, hugging sidewalks and road shoulders. Her destination this time was a shop of precious antiques. The owner advised me by phone that I might make tracks to come get her as one thump of her tail could cost me plenty in rare busted doodads.

Despite these misadventures, I let Sophie roam. I didn't want to kill her spirit, having already taken her fertility. She repaid me with her constant joy in an otherwise lonely spring.

Now and then Annie telephoned to see how we were doing. She bought a small TV and presented it to us. "I worried you might be lonely," she said as Sophie danced for the return of her prodigal mistress. "She's back! She's really back!" Sophie laughed.

But she wasn't, not really, not yet.

❧ I sat alone at a Sag Harbor pub one afternoon of Memorial Day weekend 1983. I shouldn't have ordered one wine and then another. I had a date to meet Annie at a party on a barge and didn't want to show up befuddled. I fled to the car, where Sophie waited patiently.

The barge was old and permanently parked in a slip in Accabonac Harbor in the hamlet of Springs, four miles from East Hampton. The harbor is a pristine inlet off the Great Peconic Bay with small fishing boats anchored in its coves and home to egrets, swans, and piping plovers—a favorite spot for artists and photographers and well off the beaten track from the fashionable beach crowds on the Atlantic.

At the barge, Annie waved to Sophie and me from across the deck. The May sun had tanned her and bleached her hair. Her lovely smile shone against the tan. She had finished her novel at a motel and bought a house nearby, all on her own with a loan from her family.

Noticing my fuzzy condition, Annie suggested I needed some dinner. She would cook it for me at her new house. She guided me to the barge's exit plank.

Annie's place was a vintage Springs house— a cedar shingled, two-story job with three bedrooms, two bathrooms, and a big country kitchen/dining room. It resembled Jackson Pollock's old house just down the road. The Springs area, an unincorporated hamlet, had been the headquarters for the Abstract Expressionists in the 1940s and '50s, Pollock and de Kooning (who still lived nearby) heading the list.

Annie gave me the tour. Sophie sniffed her way from room to room.

The house was mostly empty of furniture, but on the second floor, at the door to the deck, was a baby's crib, left by the previous owner, who curiously was an older lady who had no young children.

"We'll never need that," I said, pointing to the crib. "Funny she left it."

We sat on the deck, and I sipped my wine and told her about the other woman and my temptation to join her and what a great pal Sophie had been.

She regarded me, digesting the news about the other woman.

We sat silently.

"I still don't know what to say. I'm no housewife. I still have dreams for myself. The idea of a baby . . . I don't know. Alcoholism on both sides. All of it."

"We probably won't have a child. It doesn't matter. You matter, Annie. You and me and Sophie. That's all."

I put my arm around her. We kissed.

"Stop," she said, wiping away my boozy tears. "Stop."

༠ৣ The next morning I woke in Annie's house with Sophie at the foot of the bed. Annie was nowhere to be found. Then she entered the room wrapped in a beach towel. "That woman is not going to have our baby," she said. The towel dropped. "My time is perfect right now."

We went at it all week. After each session, Annie lay with her head back over the side of the bed and her feet high up the wall so that not a single sperm escaped the meeting with her single aging ovary.

"Books say every other day is best, to conserve sperm,"

I mentioned, aching and tired, on day three.

"And I say bunnies know best," Annie said.

On the seventh day, Annie too was beat. We'd done our best, I suggested. We were past her ovulation peak.

"Nope," Annie concluded. "There's probably one last egg in there. The very last one. And today's the day."

She yanked off my pants. Afterward, Annie threw her legs up against the wall. "That was the one!" she proclaimed, upside down.

Sophie laughed.

# The Sophie

## FOCAL POINT

———◆◈◆———

*Dogs are our link to paradise.*
MILAN KUNDERA

THESE WERE THE DAYS before you could run to the drugstore and get a pregnancy kit. The test got mailed off to a laboratory who then notified the doctor of the results, and finally the doctor relayed the news on to the waiting parents.

I expected nothing. The odds were so against us. I'd wait for the blood test results, which would probably be negative. If I didn't hope, I couldn't be hurt. The idea of our child– the child I had promised to my dying mother– was just that, an idea. I would stay as still as a turtle in Annie's house while we waited anxiously for the test verdict.

"The result is positive," Carol reported many weeks later, on July 19, 1983.

"Positive!" Annie shouted and leaped up.

I kissed her cheek, held her, and steadied her shaking hand. Together we hung up the phone.

Sophie, whose spaying had started it all, pranced into the room, begging a walk.

"We'll celebrate at Sophie's Beach!" Annie said.

Sophie's Beach was a long mud bank on a marshy inlet where Sophie loved to paddle. Now and then, local fishermen launched their boats there, and in the nights parked lovers used the dirt road leading up to it. But on this cool, gray evening with a drizzle falling, the three of us had it alone.

I brought along Sophie's supply of used tennis balls and a bottle of champagne. We set up a bar on the hood of the Chevy and toasted the universe while Sophie jumped off the mud banks into the bay with gigantic splashes and paddled off to retrieve thrown balls. Sophie, our child after Rocky and Ellen, our dead ersatz children.

The champagne was Annie's farewell to booze. She knocked it back, stripped down, and plunged into the inlet, naked.

"How do you feel?" I called through the drizzle.

"Incredibly high!"

Sophie splashed after more balls while Annie swam far out into the mist, her face up to the rain. I sat on the car hood and sipped.

Much later, soaking dog, towel-draped Annie, and I left Sophie's Beach in the twilight and headed toward her new house.

Everything was about to change for us. Slowly I was beginning to hope as much.

🖙 On the day before her forty-first birthday, Annie took a bus to New York for her first checkup. Carol Livoti hurried to the door. "We did it! We did it!" she said, hugging and kissing Annie. "So quickly! What did we do right?"

Then Dr. Livoti listened through her stethoscope for the new child's heartbeat. "Here. You listen," she said, handing the tip to Annie and plugging the earpieces into her ears. Annie heard the determined heartbeat, faint but definite, of her two-and-a-half-month-old child. She listened and cried while the doctor held her hand.

"It's a special baby," said Carol. "One ovary, at your age, very rare. Now we just have to make sure it stays in there."

At three months, Annie and I thought the baby would stay where it was. We could risk a romantic, Annie-cooked, candlelit, seafood pasta dinner with a half-glass of wine for Annie. And sex.

The next morning, Annie cooked her special Mississippi breakfast – eggs, ham, and grits with redeye gravy. She sang to the Gershwin on the record player.

Slowly, down the inside of her thigh, she felt a trickle then a drip. At her feet, a bloody clot formed. I helped her into a reclining chair, the same chair in which my mother had lain dying.

I struggled to reach the child inside Annie. I saw it in an epic struggle to survive, gasping, clawing, hanging on against rapids of blood. "Live! Live! Live!" I shouted.

Annie lay in Mom's old chair and prayed, "Mrs. Henderson, can you help me now? Please stop the bleeding?" Annie looked into the rising sun.

Later we phoned Dr. Livoti. She wanted us in New

York for a sonogram – a brand new device at the time. We parked Sophie with friends and set out for the city the next day.

"Hello, Mrs. McCoy, and you must be Mr. McCoy," a peppy nurse said. She led Annie to the changing room.

I was told to be seated next to a stack of family magazines featuring happy moms and pops and kids and puppies. Crippled with sorrow, I wondered if I would throw up. This was just a wake, a technical wake, for a child who had vanished.

The nurse peeked around the corner of a partition. "Mr. McCoy." She grinned. "Would you like to see your child?"

I had no idea what she was talking about. I stared at her. "Come with me." She motioned.

"Just watch the screen, Mr. McCoy," said the technician after shaking my hand. He passed an instrument over Annie's middle and pointed out the features of her womb. He mentioned something about a polyp, a bruise, and then said, "Over here, out of harm's way, here's your baby." He pointed his finger at a tiny body with a head, two legs, and two arms. Arms waving at us. The child was waving! Hello, hello!

"Hello to you too." I gulped, and then I waved back.

Later, Dr. Livoti mailed us the sonogram negatives: two sheets of eighteen black-and-white images. Our child lay in shadows on what seemed like a moonlit beach, cushioned in sand dunes.

Dr. Livoti said the sonogram was a modern marvel. A few years before this, after so much bleeding, the child might have been scraped out at a local hospital in a routine D and C operation. She called it "my sonogram baby."

❧ Annie was the amazement of her friends. "Knocked up at forty-one! Jeez, the scandal!" said Barbara Hale with a laugh. The seventy-four-year-old keeper of Springs's records, Barbara herself had been born premature. At seven months she had been left in a shoebox to die, so she swore. "They didn't think I had a chance, so they wrapped me up and put me away in the shoebox until I'd stop breathing. I fooled them!"

At parties, Annie told stories, cracked jokes, and shone gloriously. Because she was ecstatic, others were, too. Her conception of a child, against the odds, was a local wonder.

One evening, I was propped up against the bed reading with Annie with Sophie, as ever, between us. Sophie lifted her head and laid it down on Annie's belly. Together Annie and Sophie felt the flutter in her womb and were astounded at the life in her. Sophie stuck by Annie after that. Every time Annie went to lie down, Sophie would recline with her, stretching her full length against Annie's body like a guardian.

Gradually Annie began to show her pregnancy. Strangers stepped aside in line at the A&P to let her pass. People held doors open for her. Women she had never met touched her belly in appreciation.

"If only people would always treat each other like this," Annie said. For once she knew for sure she wasn't dreaming. "I know it's a cliché, but I feel like I'm the only woman in the word who ever had a baby," she exulted.

The news around us was not good: fear of nuclear holocaust had neared a universal panic. With most of the country, Annie and I watched an ABC-TV movie, *The Day After*, about the atomic end in Lawrence, Kansas. That just couldn't happen to us or our child.

The *New York Times* featured a cartoon of President Reagan brandishing a lit match in a sea of gasoline. Out in the sound, the nuclear subs prowled. We were twenty-five miles from the submarine headquarters of the country, Groton, Connecticut. Ground zero.

Carl MacIntire, nearing ninety, and still poisoning the radio, welcomed the End because that's when Jesus would judge the sinners and take Christians to heaven with Him. "Any day now," MacIntire promised. "Any day."

Annie was affected by none of this. Every day was bliss to her, and she suffered not a twinge of morning sickness. Annie was in direct contact with the world's foundation.

We were married by the justice of the peace on September 29, 1983. (Her mother had been mortified that Annie was pregnant outside of wedlock. And to a Yankee!)

Annie wore a blue ballooning dress to cover her belly and in her hair a fancy fake rose she had picked up the day before at a yard sale. Sophie came as her unadorned self.

◄§ Back when I had first brought Sophie home from the park ranger, we had posed for a photo. Sophie sat on my knees, paws curled under her, while Annie snapped the picture of our new puppy.

We are on the beach, a cool spring morning. I'm wearing her late dad's beat-up Army jacket, the one Dr. McCoy wore landing in Normandy a few days after D-day. My hair, usually flying here and there, is slicked back as if this were a formal occasion. We sit on a driftwood tree trunk. Sophie looks directly at the camera with wide-eyed innocent attention. In the background are a clear blue bay and sky, and endless white sand.

The photo is of peace and determination. After the

horror of Ellen's and Rocky's drowning, Annie and I are starting over again.

We tacked it to the wall over our bed.

During our child's birth, that photo became Annie's focal point.


In October, we endured the anxiety of an amniocentesis test – checking for deformities in the fetus, more common in women Annie's age. Again, it took weeks to hear the results. Annie and I seldom left the phone. Finally it rang.

"It's a wonderful, healthy girl!" Carol exclaimed with elation, as if she hadn't announced this to hundreds of parents before us.

At that moment, after days of darkness, sunlight saturated the tiny room.

When I was a young boy, the living room where I sat playing with Trixie was once filled with light, and I knew that God had entered that room. It's hard not to think of God's blessing when the sun shines out of a dark day at a moment like that call. Mere weather fact. A coincidence. I know.

I know.

I laugh at myself. God in the sunshine. A Hallmark card. But I can't forget it. Why at that second? Did the ringing phone rend the clouds asunder? There, that's it. A scientific explanation. The ringing phone did it.

Holly we called her – for Holy.


Dr. Livoti suggested that a modified Lamaze class might be helpful.

At the start of February, we gathered with a group of expectant parents in a fluorescent-lit room in Lenox Hill

Hospital. Our tutor was Kathy, a young, perky nurse who worked in the hospital's delivery room.

I wanted to hear only about how to get rid of Annie's pain. On the first evening, Kathy asked for a male volunteer. When no man raised his hand, she told me to stand up from my metal folding chair and come forward. "Now, Bill, if you were walking down the street and a stranger came up to you and did this, what would you do?"

Kathy balled up her fist and slammed it into my stomach, softening the blow at the last second. I bent double in reaction.

"I'd ask them what they wanted?" I tried.

Annie laughed loudly. Kathy looked at the ceiling.

"No. You would try to avoid the pain by tensing up, just as you did, which is wrong," instructed Kathy. "The point of Lamaze is that you go with the pain and not against it."

I was sent to my seat.

Going with the pain meant concentrating on regular breathing, timed contractions, and fixation on a focal point. For us that would be Sophie as a pup on the beach.

In the days before Holly's scheduled arrival it rained steadily.

Annie's womb, quiet for nine months, was suddenly not her own. Holly had gone berserk – squirming, kicking, twisting. Annie could only wait and wonder.

We waited two blocks from Lenox Hill Hospital in a suite at the Hyde Park Hotel, rented for the month of March by Annie's sister, in town for Holly's birth. No dogs allowed. Sophie languished in an East Hampton kennel.

In the Lamaze class we had become experts in dilations and contractions, but we knew nothing about infant prebirth misbehavior. So far, Holly gave no signs that she was about to allow herself to be born.

About nine o'clock, suddenly Annie developed a toothache – a molar next to her wisdom tooth. She downed a Tylenol.

The first contraction hit at 12:35 A.M. on March 14. It hit hard and it hurt bad.

The Sophie focal point was still in her suitcase. I got up to get it, but between the tooth and the contractions, she was not interested in looking at Sophie and me.

"Go with the pain, go with the pain," she coached herself and tried to follow her breathing instructions. "If this is just the start, I'm not going to finish," she told me.

Annie swallowed the next-to-last Tylenol and turned on the TV. She discovered a man with white hair, a white beard, a white suit, and a crazed stare directed at a single camera – Dr. Danny Berke and his "Trumpet of Winged Victory." He said his mission was "to save all the jerks of the world." Here was an evangelist with a twist. Not once did he mention forgiveness or sweetness. He demanded that you get your life together with Jesus or you were a twit.

Dr. Danny was assisted by a miniskirted girl who also seemed to run the single camera. She appeared from behind the camera now and then to hand him notes and newspaper clippings. In the background, on a stark all-white set, a three-piece rock band filled in when Dr. Danny ran out of outbursts.

This woke me from my semi-doze. "Who's that?" I asked Annie.

"I don't know. I just found him. He seems so sure of himself."

I watched with Annie while he plunged on into the night. Danny was her comfort, her white noise. They shared agony in the snow-quiet dark. His madness became Annie's direction. It was a place to aim the toothache, out there with Dr. Danny.

At dawn the tooth prevailed. Annie remembered the name of a dentist on Central Park South, twenty blocks away. She called. He would be in at eight. She dressed, and we attempted to walk while every six minutes a contraction bent her double. Cabs filled with rush hour passengers swarmed by. Not a chance that one would be empty. Holding on to Annie, in desperation I thrust my hand like a prayer to the sky. An empty cab braked immediately. Hoping for a safe and swift ride, I said, "My wife is having a baby." At the word baby, the driver bolted forward, dodging traffic, throwing us around in the backseat. "Jeez, a baby," he muttered, beating a red light, his eyes on Annie in the rearview mirror. Not in his cab was she going to have a baby.

The dentist was ready for us. He took a quick look at her molar and pronounced, "It's abscessed and has to come out immediately." He dialed Dr. Livoti's number. Carol said there was no way Annie could have Novocain until she checked her out.

At her office, Carol eased Annie back on the examination table and felt her abdomen with her hands. "Oh, God! She's turned on us!" Carol shouted. "Holly's turned herself completely around. Her head's straight up! It's a breech!"

Suddenly our doctor was very awake. "I don't know how to tell you this. Holly was fine ten days ago. But she made up her mind to turn. This is an emergency cesarean. There's no option."

This time it was the dentist who worried about a baby born inconveniently. He hustled Annie into his chair, injected her gum with Novocain, and yanked the tooth.

At the hospital, Annie was dressed in a gown and stretched out on a gurney to wait for the anesthesiologist, who was rushing to her side from somewhere.

A nurse followed with an iv bottle and tubes. I pinched Annie's big toes and kept on pinching hard, hoping to distract her from the pain of the needle. It did no good. "I'm sorry I forgot the Sophie focal point," I said.

We kissed, her lips puffy from the extraction, and they rolled her away to the operating room.

Carol and the others raised their hands over their heads, as if in supplication. "Ready?" she asked them.

"Excuse me," Annie said, and threw up in a bowl by her head, placed there for that very purpose.

"Ah, Chinese last night!" noted Carol. Annie nodded, smiled.

"Let's go." Carol began to cut.

She talked her way into Annie's insides.

"We are entering right above that adorable apple tattoo. Someday you will have to tell us about the night you got that tattoo," Carol joked. "We are right on top of that bikini-line scar from the cyst operation. That way you won't have two scars . . . very clean inside here . . . very clean! What a beautiful uterus, Annie! Clean as a whistle!"

She cut a bit more, moving quickly.

"There she is! I see Holly! I see her! I've got my hands on her! Oh, she's beautiful! She's beautiful!"

It was 2:32 P.M. on March 14, 1984.

And Holly was lifted into the light.

# WHAT
# Sophie Saw

*Love for a wordless creature, once it takes hold, is an
enchantment, and the enchanted speak, famously, in
private mutterings, cryptic riddles, or gibberish ... How
on earth could I stand at the requisite distance to say
anything that might matter?*

MARK DOTY

IN HIS DOG DAYS, Mark Doty was speaking of dogs but
also of children and their wordless rapture. Adults
trapped in a blizzard of words long for that rapture – that
unfettered curiosity and nonjudgmental acceptance –
and can never get it back. I had tried as a boy – with
Trixie and her ball and Duke in his golden fields. Now
Annie and I could only watch and wonder.

Back home in East Hampton, Sophie, sprung from the kennel, frantically welcomed our new child. She was very careful about Holly, but Annie was suddenly uneasy. She wanted Sophie banished to a permanent, unbreakable chain outdoors.

Annie had reason for her suspicions. Sophie had proven that she was a ruthless and adept killer of small things: a neighbor's pet duck, a friendly grouse, a passing squirrel, and years later not one but two of Holly's hamsters – pried from their cages and swallowed whole. But gradually Sophie proved to us that she was very protective of Holly and was tender with her kisses, which made Holly giggle.

Sophie lived to a respectable Labrador retriever age, and she watched Holly grow with her. Here's what Sophie saw.

&⸫ By the end of November, Holly was crawling about her playpen and standing by holding onto the bars. Holly didn't just smile for us – she grinned in an openmouthed grin of hilarity. She'd often blast herself backward with her gaaaa and lie on her back, flapping her arms like a tiny bird. She couldn't get enough of us.

Later Annie and I noticed that when the radio was on, Holly swayed to the music. For months she danced in place, supported by her parents, bobbing and bouncing, clapping her hands, interpreting any rhythm available. When, with excited giggles, she walked alone for the first time, it was more an extension of her dancing than a new skill.

She seldom merely walked – she either ran or danced, often followed by Sophie, who did fine with the running but lacked rhythm. When Holly learned how to put a tape in the stereo, Annie and I would wake to her music from the downstairs living room, soon named "The Dance Room" by Holly, where she danced in front of a floor-to-ceiling mirror.

Gershwin's *Rhapsody in Blue* was her favorite. Usually naked, she interpreted Gershwin's nuances in precise co-ordination with arms, legs, head, her whole body, bound-ing and bowing with rolls and somersaults, always with an inspiration that knew no design or choreographer.

With dance she made peace. If Annie was moody or Daddy was fussy, Holly snagged us and pulled us into her dance room, where she insisted that we twirl and jump with her. She led, we followed. There was never any excuse for not dancing. Holly hounded her reluctant par-ents from room to room. "Dance! Dance, now!"– until we gave in and spun to her lead, except for Sophie, who wanted none of it.

How did Holly know all of this? I am reminded of Wordsworth: ". . . Trailing clouds of glory do we come / From God . . ."

Holly's kisses were like Sophie's– asked for nothing, withheld no information, were given without reserva-tion, had no history or future, wanted only the moment.

Holly was always mannerly. "Dank do," she'd say when given her bottle. "Bite?" "Sip?" she'd ask, wanting to share. She'd greet a visitor to her play table: "Hi you! Comere. Sit der."

"Hurt? Hurt?" she worried, touching the shin I'd just banged or Annie's scalded finger or Sophie's stepped-on tail. In her question was the healing prayer. Once when I lay on the sofa with fever, she constructed an elaborate ceremony for me on the rug with a jump rope, a chunk of chalk, her mittens, and a magic song. It worked. In the morning I was better.

I worried about Holly's empathy for banged shins, scalded fingers, and stepped-on Sophie tails. I worried even more about the onslaught of erect boys that was only a few years away. She might be too tender for a world where kindness was a luxury.

Then I remembered the incident of the plastic scooter. Holly was about three. The scooter was bigger than she was and weighed more, too. She wanted to drag it into the house, but she couldn't fit it through the sliding glass door. A wheel caught. Normally she would have called for Daddy's help, but this matter was between herself, the scooter, and the door. She yanked, she twisted, she flipped that scooter, and she didn't complain. Some way the scooter was going in. Finally, she kicked it, and it clattered into the house.

I saw that there was a core within Holly that was not to be messed with, by scooter or human.

One day that same year, she learned the importance of her name.

"Hey, kid!" I called as she dashed across the yard.

She stopped, hands on hips. "Name's Holly!" she yelled.

"OK, OK, Holly," I agreed, and never called her "kid" again lightly.

Soon the "Holly" was joined to a last name. "Name's Holly Hunnerson," she told guests as she regarded them eye to eye.

And there was even more for her to be proud about two months later.

"Guess what, Daddy."

"I give up. What?"

"I'm a girl!" she shouted.

This was real news, and she knew it immediately. Huge news. Holly. Holly Hunnerson. A girl! And tough enough to kick a scooter through a door without apologies.

 I decided that Holly needed her own dog, like my Trixie, a pal she could call hers. Sophie had ruled comfortably for many years, but she was an eighty-five-pound behemoth. It was time for her to move over.

Charlie was Holly's first and lamentable dog. He was a dachshund, my surprise Christmas present. The breed came highly recommended, a small dog, like Trixie, that Holly could wrestle with, toss a ball to.

So in the days before Christmas I rummaged through the newspaper ads and found a dealer up island, a breeder of champion dachshunds.

She lived down a dirt road in a trailer. Her dogs, dozens of them, resided in her house. She unlocked her front door and gave me the tour. The odor was rather special. Pee and poop had not recently been picked up. The dogs did not seem all that thrilled to see me.

In the bathroom, down a long, dark hall, was a recent litter of round, stubby-legged puppies. I picked one in haste, gagging and desperate for air, gave her a $375 check, and sped back down the road to East Hampton. It was only a few days before Christmas, and I didn't have much of a choice in the dachshund market. He lay in the backseat like a lump of brown clay.

At home I made the grand presentation: "Ta ta! Holly! Your own puppy, your Christmas puppy! Merry Christmas!" I held forth the lump for her examination.

She didn't know what to make of it.

"You should have gift-wrapped him, Bill – at least tied a ribbon around his neck," suggested Annie, who was a genius at appropriate ceremonies.

I set the dog on the rug, and he immediately decorated it with a copious spew of diarrhea.

We named him Charlie – why, I don't know. Perhaps after Prince Charles.

Events only went downhill from there. I'd been assured that Charlie had been "vet checked" and healthy, but he had no spunk, no fire in his long belly. He wandered about the house like a large worm, crapping and peeing when he felt like it.

I tried all the tricks for housebreaking: scolding for inside mistakes, high loud praise for occasional outside evacuations. Charlie responded to both with his dull stare.

As I have said, with all my dogs I prefer to have discussions. By looking deep into their eyes and speaking with a slightly raised voice, I eventually reach an understanding with them about proper deportment.

Not with Charlie.

We were at the top of the stairs when I lost it. After almost a month of begging him to understand, he delivered a dump at my feet. I swept him aside so I could clean it up, and he rolled over and over down the entire stairwell. I was horrified that I'd killed him. Not so. He looked up at me from the foot of the stairs with the same numb eyes.

Back to the lady in the trailer he went. No refund. Not Charlie's fault, I know. House was where all his pals crapped. The trailer was the lady's toilet. House dumping was bred in the bone.

I've never forgotten Charlie's blank eyes. Or was it aristocratic disdain?

Holly didn't seem to miss him, never brought it up. Sophie, I'm sure, was glad to see him gone.

Holly, like her mom, loved a joke. Any joke. Her humor was far more scatological than I had been permitted as a boy. One morning we all lay in the summer predawn darkness and heard a bird begin to sing. The bird was creating an elaborate song, really working out, when he seemed to notice that he was all alone. The bird shut up and sang no more.

"Holly," I said, "that bird got up too early. He made a dope of himself. Now he's sitting out there in the dark all embarrassed and red-faced."

Holly hooted and farted under the covers. Because of the fart, she hooted and farted again. She ran out of the room hooting and farting and hooting at the red-faced bird and her own flatulence.

Sophie, it should be noted, had no toleration for her own farts. If she blasted while sleeping, she woke and dashed out of the room in chagrin. Holly thought that was hilarious. Sophie didn't get the joke.

Holly would sometimes sit on the toilet, thinking, while I shaved. While in her thinking spot one day, she said, "Sometimes I wonder what it's like to be another person."

"I wonder about that, too," I said. "I wonder what it's like to be you, Holly."

"What's it like to be you, Daddy?"

I put my razor down. Looking at her in the mirror, I attempted an answer. "Well, most days I work at Pushcart Press in the garage. I make phone calls. Think up ideas for books. Write in my journal. Pack books in boxes."

"Oh," she said, reaching for the toilet paper.

"That's a very good question you asked, Holly."

Holly looked at me, flushed the toilet, and left without comment, perhaps already on to the next wonder, perhaps disappointed by my lame answer.


᭟᧥ As Holly grew and my finances did not, I worried about college and how to pay for it. I developed a scheme: I'd build a summer cabin in Maine and rent our East Hampton house from June to Labor Day to the Hampton-crazed folks from New York. Rents were ridiculously high. I'd deposit the funds into Holly's college account.

With no building experience, besides a tree fort and a doghouse, and only a book of basics to help me, Sophie and I set off one spring for a little plot of island land I had purchased on Deer Isle. I had a cement slab laid and got to work, with Sophie as my only companion through lonely days of rain, sun, mosquitoes and black flies, and tough weeks of fourteen-hour days. I used no power tools – just a hammer, saw, square, level, tape measure, and rope.

Sophie watched it all with bemusement. I wondered what she would have done if I fell off my ladder? Run for help like King? Most likely she would have just licked my face to make it better, barked for aid, and – if nothing else helped – had me for dinner.

But I didn't fall, and in two months, with some local help, I'd framed, sheathed, and roofed a substantial cabin for our family, complete with flush plumbing, a shower, electricity, a screened porch, a chimney, and a roof that did not leak.

For the next few years we collected hefty Hampton rents for Holly's education and lived in the Maine summertime woods.

~§ One August night on our Maine island, Annie, Holly, Sophie, and I drove to a hilltop cemetery to watch the annual Perseid shooting star showers. We lay on the blanket and stared upward together into the clear, cold sky.

It wasn't a great night for shooting stars, but the crickets were berserk with song.

"Sometimes I hear crickets sing and sing, and then I sleep and they stop. I wake up because I can't hear them anymore. It's so quiet I wonder what happened to them," Holly commented.

We listened some more. "How do crickets sing, Dad?"

"Well, they rub their legs together– "

"But how does that make music?"

Long ago I had wondered about that too. But time had passed, and I forgot to wonder, just as time rushed over the people buried in this cemetery and over the three of us sitting on this hillside watching for brief, sudden passages of light.

"I don't know," I said.

~§ "Dad, what will people say we did?" Holly asked me one afternoon. Her class had just visited the town marine museum and its farming and fishing artifacts.

I had no answer. One hundred years from now, what would we have left behind? "They'll say we drove cars, had children, lived in houses– "

"No. What will they say we did?" I had no answer.

But afterward, her question wouldn't leave me. Farm,

fish? No, I decided. We bought and sold stuff– that was the answer. All was for sale, all we cared about. Would we leave behind plows and fishing gear? No. Only stuff– and lots of electronic gizmos.

People might note our ridiculous celebrity worship and our busyness that never changed as we rushed from place to place and fired off empty electronic messages.

Holly, I could have said, they might say we did nothing at all.

◆§ In the years since Holly was born, every lot on our long East Hampton street, formerly empty, was occupied by cheap, faux-modern houses, most with T-1-11 plywood siding and fake salt box roof lines. With each house arrived two or three cars. The town was becoming a noisy parking lot.

Too late the town reacted, creating reserves such as the Grace Estate that I bicycled through with my backpack on my daily way to the post office. Here I could dream that I was back in the empty woods of years ago, the land of Jackson Pollock, Irwin Shaw, Truman Capote, James Jones, Willy Morris– when "Hamptons" meant art and literature, not just plain awful money.

One winter day at the funky, little rundown airport, I was joined in my postal bicycle mission by a dog– a furry fellow who came out of nowhere and loped easily next to me. He ran just for the joy of the lope, not insisting that I stop and play or even acknowledge him. For a mile or two he maintained my pace, and I was glad to have a companion. Finally I stopped and talked to him, suggesting he might go home before he got lost. He smiled and stayed put, a big guy, maybe a cross between a Shetland sheepdog and a Great Dane. He had no tags.

He just has to get tired soon, I figured, remounting my bike. But Airport, for that's what I called him, never slowed his jovial pace over six miles. We became a team, racing through the last of the East Hampton woods, past the swimming pool where Ellen and Rocky died— now a fenced and landscaped summer paradise sold long ago for a stunning profit.

At home, Airport was a wonderfully accommodating fellow. Even Sophie seemed to like him. He loved for people to hug his huge, hairy self. At Christmas he was in all the videos we took. Sophie and Airport, always helping unwrap presents, woofing at what popped out of boxes.

Had he been abandoned at the airport by tourists? Some of them just dumped their cats and dogs at season's end. But it was December. I called the dog warden, notified ARF, advertised in the "Found" section of the East Hampton Star.

Finally, weeks later, his owner knocked on the door, a friend of a friend told him where Airport was. "I wondered where he'd gotten to," he said but didn't seem all that excited to see his dog again. Airport, ever helpful, jumped into his car and was driven away.

I never found out his real name.

We all wish he had stayed.

&ᴣ From time to time, Holly rebelled. For instance, she found it intolerable that adults made you sit through boring dinners and wouldn't let you eat SpaghettiOs. Annie insisted on combed hair and neat clothes.

Daddy was a fanatic about brushing teeth. One night it all became too much, and Holly kicked her foot against the wall, smashing clear through the wallboard. She hadn't known she was that strong and ran off to hide in a closet upstairs, terrified. "Gosh, you're strong," I said, comforting her and coaxing her out.

Another night she fled from the adults into a rainy night, screaming, "I hate you, I hate you both, and I always will . . . but I still love you."

Foot through the wall, screams in the rain. Even Holly at her worst was sensual.

Until Holly was born, I didn't realize what true sensual joy was – watching your child grow up, learning from her again how to dance and kiss and make magic and laugh at silly jokes and fall into rapture about shooting stars and wonder about how crickets sing and strut with pride at your sex and your very own name.

And above all, to be constantly and forever amazed.

Love is a word that only children and dogs say truly. For the rest of us, love is corrupted every day by a cynical culture and our own never-ending qualifications.

To Holly, love was as real as a rock. Her "I love you, Momma, Poppa, Sophie" before sleeping was offered without reservations, like her kiss.

At night, after I read her a bedtime story, I'd see her drifting off to sleep, and I didn't want her to leave.

"You're a great kid, kid," I said.

"You're a great dad, Dad," she said, curling up.

Please don't sleep, Holly, I whispered to myself. We have so few days together. Don't go to that other place. Stay with me a few minutes more.

Once, lying on the floor by her bed, I dreamed that she was on a subway train in a slum, and I couldn't find out what train or where the train was taking her through the night. I woke up yelling in terror with Annie shaking me.

Now and then I'd stare at Holly in wonder. Her gentle face, her grace. Obviously God was a woman, I'd imagine.

Then I'd wonder at my wonder. Why didn't I spend every moment in amazement at her – at everybody? How could the life of a child, or any life, become ordinary? Another drive to the nursery school, another snapping in of a kid's video on the VCR, another evening meal? How could I allow any second to be routine?

With Holly's friends, affection was never muted. They didn't need a boozy cocktail party or a church moment of peace to inspire a kiss. Their love for each other was a matter of every moment. To walk down the street holding hands or with their arms around each other wasn't a bit remarkable. Love was the way it was for them; the moon, the stars, everything.

In Maine a few summers ago, I'd had a rough day: in the mail, lousy reviews for a recent Pushcart title and an agent's crabby letter.

I stood alone on a rock, looking out to sea. Nearby, Holly piled up a sandcastle using a clamshell for a shovel. She glanced up, saw my face, dropped her shell, and walked over to me. Silently she leaned against my leg, watching the sea, a quiet support.

"Try not to worry, Dad."

"OK, Holly. I'll only worry about you."

"I love you, Daddy."

"That's good to know."

"But you already know that!" she scolded, astonished that I could have forgotten. And angry.

"You're right. I'm sorry," I said, feeling very stupid.

Later that day we canoed on Lily Pond, and I tried to

tell Holly about the life and death of my mother, but I choked up and couldn't continue. I pretended to be interested in a beaver dam across the pond. We paddled toward it.

"Did Grandma Henderson know me before she died?" she asked.

"No. But I told her I was hoping you would be born someday. She would have loved you."

We sat in the canoe for a while, waiting for beavers in the still pond.

Patient, caring, a teacher – my mother was like Holly. In 1942, my father had constructed a record-maker in the basement and recorded my mother and him putting their kids to bed.

One night Annie and I listened to that scratchy record, and then we watched Annie's videotape of us doing the same thing. The children's voices, the adult responses, were almost identical. Is this what Jesus meant by immortality? What's done with love endures? I remember my mother's calls to see if I was OK; I hear the evening birdsong, see the quiet twilight.

Holly completed the circle.

When Holly was very young, I tried to tell her about Christmas. I said it was a birthday party for a kind man named Jesus who lived long ago and said the most important rule of all was that we love God and love each other just as much as we love ourselves. I stumbled on that word love, had to dig my nails into my palms.

Holly looked at me brightly. "Jesus needs a birthday present. How about a Mr. Potato Head?"

Annie appreciated tradition. To her, church was ceremonies, songs, pageantry, and Sunday outfits. She wanted Holly to know these traditions. So she dressed her up and enrolled her in the Sunday school of the tiny nearby Presbyterian church, no bigger than a storefront with an old steeple that slanted toward the rear as if about to crash down on the congregation.

"Where's Mr. Henderson?" the Irish minister asked at the coffee hour. "That's a good Presbyterian name."

But I was having none of his church. The idea of walking through a church door after decades of absence evoked astonishing dread. Perhaps I thought I'd meet my father there. I'd have to deal all over again with his shyness and silence. Shades of Carl McIntire! I had contempt for church doctrine and all who believed such tales. How brain-dead they seemed! Miracles! The Son of God! The Resurrection! Had they ever once thought about any of it? How annoying– and horrifying– that they might welcome me back with their Christian grins.

On the night of February 25, 1990, our part of Long Island was entombed by a record blizzard. Not much moved on Sunday morning, and the town's plows managed to cut only a narrow lane to the village center past the church.

My usual Sunday morning ritual was common: a bagel and coffee in bed with the *New York Times* and a walk with Sophie. But outside I could see no *Times* delivered on the mounds of snow that were increasing by the minute. Sophie regarded the weather morosely.

"We're off to church!" Annie announced through the door to the bathroom, where I sat on the toilet contemplating a *Times*-less morning.

"You can't drive down there!" I yelled through the door.

"Yes, I can!" she called back.

In seconds I reasoned that I had to get hold of a *Times* to survive the morning in good habit and that I could also chauffeur Holly and Annie safely to church. I'd buy a *Times* at the general store, read it there, and pick them up after services.

But why not go into the church too?

A Zen monk once admitted that he received several enlightenments while evacuating of a morning. Doing the same, I pondered why I was so afraid of church. I pulled up my pants, found a tie, and we spun off into the blizzard.

The windshield wipers were frozen down. I couldn't free them. I did manage to clear a spot in the windshield, but the wet snow quickly covered it. So I drove like a train engineer with my head out the window, very slowly, wiping my eyes with a handkerchief Annie handed me.

With Holly and Annie, I walked through the church door into a mostly empty room. Sunday school was canceled. The organist was snowed in, and only a dozen people who lived close by had turned out. The minister with his Santa Claus white beard carried us in song without the organ. Simple, tentative voices. I heard quiet people trying to carry a tune about a Lord who they hoped would save them somehow from private pain, dread, sorrow, confusion.

During the service, I was singled out by the minister as the stranger in the group and, as was the custom there, was asked to explain who I was and how I came to be there.

I stood next to Holly and Annie and said, "I attended a Philadelphia Presbyterian church a long time ago.

Today I got here with my head out the car window because the windshield wipers were stuck and I couldn't see the road."

The people laughed.

What happened next is still happening. Since I was a boy I had longed for somebody to talk to me about the church, as my worshiping but silent father had been unable to do so. The Irish minister loved to talk. The Bishop of Blarney, I nicknamed him. We became friends.

The man said Holly's word love in sermons. He and his congregation sang that word. They promised they loved each other and God. Holly's word seemed real to them, too, as real as a rock. And with that word I imagined they honored the other words that follow from it: awe, wonder, mystery, joy. Holly's other virtues.

Strange words in a poisoned world.

These people confessed that they were like little children.

I saw them as revolutionaries.

The next week, the Sunday *Times*, which had been there all along, emerged from the melting drift. The front page headlined, "The Universe Is Strangely Ordered, Scientists Find." Holly and I built a huge snow fort from the drift with a front and back door, windows, and a roof so high you could sit up inside.

Friends worried that in my affection for the church I only longed for my past. Not nostalgia, I said. My very soul, hidden for years.

Here at last was my answer to Holly's question: "What's it like to be you, Dad?"

When I joined the church again in November 1990, Annie and Holly heard me lie a bit: "I accept Jesus as my savior," I promised the congregation. But I crossed my fingers and substituted "Love" for "Jesus." Only love saves us. I think Jesus appreciated my qualifications.

In that moment the wordless soul of Sophie and all the dogs of my life guided me. As Jon Katz observed, "Sometimes dogs show us the way back."

# Opie

*The great pleasure of a dog is that you may make
a fool of yourself with him and not only will he not
scold you, but he will make a fool of himself too.*
SAMUEL BUTLER

OPIE WAS A rescue beagle – rescuing not him but rather his elderly owners. We rescued them from his howling, sniffing, irrepressible self.

Opie was about three years old, brown and white, tending to pudgy. When Holly and I heard that he needed a new playground, we set out to see him, promising Annie it would only be a temporary adoption if she disapproved, to help our friends the elderly couple.

At the time I was off my evening cocktail habit and

was flooded with the excessive energy of the newly tee-totaled. I needed a project. I knew nothing about beagles besides what I'd read in the Peanuts cartoons. Snoopy was a smart, opinionated fellow, his own dog. I liked that. Besides, Holly still lacked her own Trixie dog, after the failure of numb Charlie, and Opie was exactly the right size. She fell for him at first sight.

This turned out to be no temporary adoption. Opie stayed for a long time. If he kept out of her (our) bed, Sophie let him be. But they never played. Opie adored Sophie, but it was unrequited adoration.

Opie's problem was his nose. He was a slave to it. Like Ellen, he did not discriminate among multiple passions – all senses that originated in his nose he followed with enormous dedication. Smell to smell, he howled down the beaches and through the Maine forests. The idea of tracking just one odor never occurred to him. Opie was a kaleidoscope of ever-changing olfactory impulses. And always that howl.

A Maine neighbor remarked politely, "He's very noisy. And just remember local people around here don't forget." I never figured out what that meant– damage to our cabin in the winter, a shotgun for Opie. Bizarre that in Maine, with miles of wilderness, Opie could cause such discomfort with his nose.

Virginia Woolf, in her fictional biography of Flush, Elizabeth Barrett Browning's spaniel, goes right up his nose:

> *Up the funnel of the staircase came warm whiffs of joints roasting, of fowls basting, of soups simmering – ravishing almost as food itself . . . Mixing with the smell of food*

*were further smells – smells of cedarwood and sandal*
*wood and mahogany; scents of male bodies and female*
*bodies; of men servants and maid servants; of coats and*
*trousers; of crinolines and mantles; of curtains of tapes-*
*try, of curtains of plush; of coal dust and fog; of wine and*
*cigars. Each room as he passed it – dining-room, draw-*
*ing-room, library, bedroom – wafted out its own cont-*
*ribution to the general stew.*

Opie lived a rich life in his nose, but to me he was useless. I wanted a dog to hike and bike with me, like Duke
or Airport and now Sophie. Opie had no interest in such
lame exercises. There were millions of smells to track
down. The orgasmic joy of it!

To Holly he was her dream dog. She ignored his nose
fixations and entertained him inside with her friends.
Opie danced for them. He loved the music, the attention,
and the ladies. He switched partners and danced and
danced on two feet to whatever was hot in the eight-year-
old music scene. Sometimes he lost it in ecstasy. He
couldn't contain his frenzied rhythm, and instead he
humped a pillow in sexual abandon while the girls boo-
gied on without him. (Note: Stravinsky said, "Only children and animals understand my music.")

Holly loved Opie because he was so conceited, so
ridiculously stuck-up, "a really strong person," but she
was not blind to his failings: when not howling, he
clucked like a chicken, and he was distinguished by
strong odor. She remembers he always smelled like a wet
dog.

A regal wet dog. When Holly and friends dressed him
in a purple cloak and cardboard crown and sat him on a

finely upholstered chair and sprinkled rose petals before him, hailing "King Opie! King Opie!" he seemed to know this was his due and his station in life.

Then he'd jump off his throne and play hide-and-seek or cuddle on the couch or mightily howl at whoever was at the door, including me. He was Holly's marvelous, cranky buddy.

But the howling got to me and more of our Maine neighbors. For miles he'd roam, always announcing his latest smell at top singing voice. The neighbors had had it.

Our family took a vote. We decided that Opie was too much for us. He would be happier further off in the country.

Holly was unhappy but OK with that. She only wanted the best for her friend.

A man and his wife answered our ad in the *Deer Isle Ad-vantages*. I tried to warn them that Opie was a two-time loser. We were the second owners he had driven nuts. But the man said, "He just needs training. I'll hunt with him. I know how to handle beagles."

"Well, if it doesn't work out, just call me and I'll pick him up," I offered.

We waved good-bye to a perplexed but still regal Opie in the back of their disappearing pickup truck.

The next morning a 7:00 A.M. the phone rang. "That damn dog tried to kill my cats and crapped all over our shag rug. Come get him."

Opie was back on his throne.

Opie was the first to know that Sophie had died. Suddenly at 10:09 that July morning in 1992, he sat on his lead outside and sang sadly into the air, not about scent this time but about the death of his adored mentor. He would not stop his mourning wails.

Sophie had been failing all that summer, losing weight, dehydrated. She wouldn't retrieve – in fact, she could barely walk. She had begun to hide herself on the floor of the car.

I had to carry her into the Blue Hill animal hospital, where we had been often before. "Please do what you can for her," I asked.

The vet wasn't too promising. "I think we'd better help her out," he mentioned.

I concentrated on "help" and not "out" and drove back to the cabin. He called me early the next day. "She's dying. I'd better ease her away. Would you like to be here?"

I declined, too much for me to bear. I couldn't watch Sophie, savior of our little family, let go of her great soul. We had all said our farewells the night before, she not comprehending where she was or who we were.

Opie sensed far more than what his nose told him. He knew the instant his adored friend died miles away that summer morning.

"Why is Opie howling like that?" asked Annie.

Then we knew.

We spread Sophie's ashes on the pond outside the cabin and on Sophie's Pond, where she had often cooled off. Holly composed a poem, and we all said a prayer for the Labrador retriever who changed it all for us, our comfort after Ellen and Rocky died, the keystone of our fragile family, and Annie's focal point for Holly's birth.

As John Grogan wrote of Marley,

*He became part of our melded fabric, a tightly woven
and inseparable strand in the weave that was us. Just as
we had helped shape him into the family pet he would
become, he helped to shape us, as well – as a couple, as
parents, as animal lovers, as adults. Despite everything,
all the disappointments and unmet expectations, Marley
had given us a gift, at once priceless and free. He taught
us the art of unqualified love.*

⋘ It was Opie's house now.

A few days later he took Sophie's place on our bed.

Opie was the first and only dog we had owned who
arrived with proper AKC papers. They announced that
he was Son of Bruno, the Duke of Eqununk, and Lady
Sand Pebbles III. And don't you forget it.

Now that Queen Sophie was gone, King Opie suddenly realized he was no longer a pretender to the real
throne, and he became even more haughty and opinionated. But his nose would be his ruin.

First, though, he helped me build a tower on a Maine
hill.

I had never heard of Christy Hill in Sedgwick until
February 1995, when a local real estate agent, aware of
my interest in land with a water view, and with sympathy
for my limited bank account, mailed me a grainy photo-
copy of a small lot with distant views of the ocean glit-
tering like a thin string of light on the horizon. Not very
promising, I thought, but I needed the drive to Maine
and the infusion of energy that I always get from the stu-
pendously beautiful Down East coast.

I had just finished writing about my daughter's birth

eleven years before and about how Holly, in her growing up, had taught her dad all he had once known but forgotten.

After years of being written, more of being rewritten (every comma had to be correct, every memory exact), and many rejections, my memoir had finally been accepted by a publisher in Boston. I drove there, delivered the manuscript to Faber and Faber, and headed north to Maine with Opie by my side, the balance of Faber's modest advance check in my pocket. I needed to see Maine again. I was emptied out. And my daughter was no longer a child; our baby didn't need her dad as much anymore. Memoir finished, baby gone, I felt hollow inside. Restless. Perhaps more depressed than I realized.

The real estate agent gave me general directions to Christy Hill. I asked for help at the Sedgwick general store and was told to circle the Baptist church and head straight up. Since the hill is almost 400 feet high, I expected a dramatic rise from sea level, but my ascent was a gradual one of soft inclines and plateaus through a mixed forest of spruce and maple, beech and birch.

Up I drove for another mile until the road peaked in an expanse of blueberry fields. Hearing my rackety car, three deer bounded across the white fields. The sun's glare off the snow made it hard to see, but finally I spotted the broker's sign that marked the lot, swinging on its hinges in the wilderness.

I stopped the car, and Opie and I got out to look around. In the clear cold air to the northeast was the crown of Blue Hill, lofting over Blue Hill village at its base, scene of the annual Blue Hill Fair. Twenty miles to the east across Blue Hill Bay were the mountains of Acadia National Park, and below me were Swans Island and dozens of lesser islands and ledges, fringed with ice. Beyond them the open ocean stirred quietly.

I walked through the woods 160 feet to the stone wall at the rear of the lot, where I discovered more acres of blueberry fields and, miles away, light fog rising off the Penobscot River and, still farther in the distance, the mountains of the northwest.

Opie had taken off after a scent, wrecking the stillness. I sat on that old stone wall for a long time, stunned by this sacred place.

There was no way I could afford it, I thought. My advance would cover only a portion of the asking price. Besides, what was this really but a 1.78-acre subdivision in the middle of nowhere?

More importantly, how could I explain this infatuation to my wife? Annie might point out that we already had the summer cottage on Deer Isle that I had spent years building obsessively. No way did we need another lot in Maine, she'd say, perhaps rising to operatic hyperbole about my edifice complex. She might remind me that we often couldn't pay our bills, particularly that fuel bill last winter. She would bring to my attention my dying Oldsmobile station wagon with more than 160,000 miles on the odometer, held together with duct tape. And I'd have to admit that while Pushcart Press had become an institution – with dozens of titles on its list and the Pushcart Prize being proclaimed by the *New York Times Book Review* as "a distinguished annual literary event" – the press had been hanging on by its financial fingernails for twenty-three years. Frequently I had relied on a cash miracle or the kindness of friends to bail it out.

"What would I do with this lot?" I asked Opie and myself on that wall.

I called my friend, critic and author Doris Grumbach, at her bookstore nearby. She and her partner, Sybil, had lived here more than a decade. I invited Doris to church, and after church I drove her to the top of Christy Hill and pointed out the distant views across the fields.

"What are you going to do here?" Doris asked.

"I don't know. Probably leave it as it is. It's perfect. No houses, no people, wild."

Doris, who is always careful with her words, said nothing.

In my mind suddenly was a vision of a tower on a moonlit cliff– right out of some forgotten nineteenth-century romantic English novel that my parents or grandparents might have read. I didn't tell Doris about my vision. She might have questioned my taste, if not my sanity. A nineteenth-century tower? What could that possibly mean?

"Maybe I'll build a tower here." I laughed and started the car.

⋙ With the last of our miniscule savings, I bought the Christy Hill lot. I'd explain to Annie later, I hoped.

Since I couldn't dig my foundation until the April thaw, Opie and I drove back to East Hampton and announced our purchase. Annie said nothing, perhaps exhausted with her husband's erratic visions.

I dreamed of towers, a jumble of spires, but still couldn't forget that original and persistent nineteenth-century epiphany with Doris, a solid spire rooted to a dark hill. I imagined the sea smashing on distant islands, clouds racing over Acadia toward the western mountains, and, straight up, the full moon, the stars, galaxies, the ultimate forever.

There would be no neighbors near this tower with their petty busynesses and no petty busynesses of my own either. And no distracting black flies or mosquitoes (which is quite an omission in buggy Maine, but I recall that Wordsworth left bugs out of his nature rhapsodies, too). Just me and the wild turkeys, coyotes, moose, porcupines, skunks, deer, eagles, and black bears – Smith's Pond again, the Ocean City marshes, the Austin Estate. Uncompromised. At full attention. Lifted up. Nearer to the eternal spirit. Brother of Thoreau. Child of Holly.

But then there was vertigo. Until now, in my dreaming, I had ignored this neurotic malfunction. As a kid, I could scramble up any tree without a care, but now I couldn't climb open stairs a few stories without clawing for support and inching back down on my hands and knees. The vistas from the tops of the great steeples and monuments of Europe and America were unknown to me.

My vertigo was not of the dizzy variety. It was worse. I had topple-down vertigo. At heights I was driven to pitch myself forward into the air.

I'd have to deal with the vertigo some other way. I had no idea what way. That could wait while I handled more immediate difficulties, like building alone.

Because I couldn't afford to pay for help, and my wife was no builder and had no interest in towers of any ilk, I was going to be one guy with a dog and lots of lumber and cement to haul into the woods, which as yet had no road, no driveway, not even a path. And after I chose my site and assembled my materials, I would have to raise it all alone and by hand.

As for electricity, a line through the sweet woods from the poles at the dirt road? Never. No television, no computer, no e-mail, no fax, no phone. I would be blessedly out of the hypnotic national electronic loop.

And no gasoline machinery, either. No generators, no backhoes, no cranes, I pledged. Bad enough that I drove that smoking Oldsmobile. Someday, it too would go. Then I would rediscover my feet by hiking up and down this magnificent hill, with Opie on a leash.

⤳ "Simplify, simplify," said Thoreau about building his Walden Pond cabin, and a few paragraphs later he repeated, "Simplify, simplify, simplify." Note: to be truly simple, he might have said the word just once.

Simple. My tower, I finally decided after much deliberation, would be a box on top of a box. A box on top of a box, and, if I were daring, yet another box on top of that box, and so forth into the clouds. Sort of a plain Quaker tower – although, as far as I knew, Quakers erected no towers.

All that summer I labored at my Quaker tower, while Holly bunked at a camp on a nearby lake and Annie finished a novel in our Deer Isle cabin. Opie stood guard when he felt like it, and every noon Annie arrived with lunch she'd prepared, demanding that we take a break.

By summer's end I had framed and sheathed the tower, installed the various windows, and by November, defying chronic vertigo, I had tacked and tarred the roofing and nailed down an observation deck with views for miles out to sea. Later I'd write a memoir about all this: *Tower: Faith, Vertigo, and Amateur Construction* with detailed how-to instructions and an after-the-fact budget, like Thoreau's for his Walden cabin.

As the first snows drifted past, I wrapped it all in blue tarpaulin, like a Christo artwork, and left it to the worst of winter winds.

Opie and I headed south. He never saw Maine again.

⋅⋅⋅ Because East Hampton traffic had become horrendous, and Opie chose to ignore cars, we almost never let him run loose there. But on that June day of 1995, while I was in my studio packing up papers for the annual Maine summer migration, he had been left out for a second, sleeping on the back step.

The phone rang. Annie whispered frantically to me so Holly in the next room couldn't hear. "Hurry, hurry, hurry, Opie's lying in the road."

In minutes I was there. Opie lay on the usually quiet side street, covered with a towel, a splash of blood next to his head. A guy in a truck had turned the corner, probably doing only ten or fifteen miles an hour on the curve, and hit him. Opie could have easily dodged the truck, but he was, after all, Opie, respected senior dog, age nine, with all his AKC papers and a new and important scent to attend to. He had been killed instantly.

"I hit him. I hit him hard!" said the distraught driver to Annie at the back door. "I never saw him." There was no use trying to revive Opie. Annie told the driver it wasn't his fault, and he drove away.

Annie was afraid that Holly would be ruined by the news. But when we told her, she was calmer than we were, upset, but trying first of all to quiet our grief. I carried Opie's body to the backyard. Holly uncovered his head, his eyes still frantic for that last scent, and for a long time she sat petting his damaged body while I dug a grave in the little woods out back.

As she had for Sophie, Holly made formal funeral arrangements. She bundled up all his toys, leash, snacks, and his favorite pillow. We wrapped him in a sheet and a plastic bag in a fetal position; put sheet, bag, and body in the grave atop his pillow; and together shoveled in the dirt. Holly fashioned a cross above his grave inscribed, "Here lies Opie. He loved to dance."

⋖§ In his magnificent *Merle's Door*, Ted Kerasote remembers his own dancing dog, Merle. This passage describes wonderfully what Opie was for Holly. It takes place while Merle is in his last year. I can't read it without choking up.

> *I put some country-western music on the CD player and tapped my chest with my palms, he'd stand on his hind legs, put his front paws on my shoulders, and we'd dance around the great room together while he panted, "This is fun!" Sometimes, he'd even come and find me if some bluegrass music began to play on the radio, jumping off the dedicated quadruped couch, trotting into the office, wagging his tail, and pumping his paws up and down, indicating, "Let's dance."*

After Merle died, Kerasote looked to the empty corner of the room where he had slept. He goes on to explain his pilgrimage to Merle's grave:

> *I . . . walked to his grave, where I stood, listening to the hum of the river and feeling the universe still pressed out to its farthest corners by him. And I couldn't tell if the bigness was him or how we had filled each other's hearts*

*or if there was any difference between the two. Looking down, I imagined him lying on his green bed. Even though he would now always be close, it seemed like too confined an end for a dog who liked to roam. I needn't have worried. When I looked up, he was bounding across the grass toward me, already as much starlight as dog. Tail lashing, front paws dancing, he twirled before me.*

*"You dance, Sir!" I cried.*

*"Ha-ha-ha!" he panted. "I dance! I DANCE!"*

~ Holly and Annie sank into tearful and silent gloom. "We long for something to make sense and be simple, just like childhood, that sweet innocence. That's why it hurts so bad," Annie said.

I'm no good at sorrow, can't stand it, must do something, anything, to make it go away. That split-second chance encounter between a truck tire and his plump, vibrant body– that can't be. It was the death of Ellen and Rocky all over again. What to do? Scream? Curse God? Drink? No house to burn down this time. No fault except Opie's innocence.

For more than twelve years we had never been dogless. The emptiness was overwhelming. No yips, licks, patter of paws. My answer: get another dog now. Somewhere a dog was feeling the same hollow horror we were. That dog and our family needed each other. The next morning I set out alone to find that dog.

I drove to ARF.

THE HYMN OF

## Lulu & Max

*A really companionable and indispensable dog is an
accident of nature. You can't get it by breeding and you
can't buy it with money. It just happens along.*
E.B. WHITE

EVERYBODY HAS A few moments in their life when they
feel the Great Spirit, God, or the Great Coincidence is in
control. Things come together. A terrible death, sudden
new life. At ARF I found that life in a homely, triumphant
mutt named Chewy, after the shaggy Star Wars character.
For the next decade we would almost never be apart.

Chewy had been at the shelter for more than a year,
unclaimed, unloved – a single mom, spayed now. Had
her profligate motherhood driven her from her previous
home? About two years old? Nobody knew for sure.

She was about eighty-five pounds of shagginess. Perhaps a committee had pieced her together – a German shepherd face, floppy dreadlocked Afghan ears, a golden retriever body. Her face and muzzle said ferocious, her eyes indicated kind, her tail wagged like a puppy's for friend and stranger alike.

I first saw Chewy as I drove up to the ARF compound. She was being walked by a couple of prospective owners. Up and down the driveway they went while I watched. Something about her fascinated me. Later I remembered she had been the lead dog in East Hampton's annual Santa parade, ARF division. Chewy, in a red bandanna, had led her pack of abandoned dogs down the center of Main Street, on a leash, her head held high, not haughty, just not dejected. (Thanks to the local television station, I have a copy of their video of that long-ago parade, and there she is, just as I recalled.) Sitting in my car, I hoped desperately the couple would pass her over so I could walk her. They did. I ran in, asked the attendant for permission to walk the shaggy dog, and off we went together for our first hike.

I have known few animals – and fewer humans – with such a natural, unself-conscious dignity. She accepted me and I her with no question. We walked and thought in tandem. Back at the ARF office, I asked for permission to take Chewy home for an overnight, so Holly and Annie could approve of her. I filled out some papers, made a small donation. She walked alongside me to the car, and I opened the door. She looked back at me. "You want me to get in?" she asked with her eyes. "Go ahead, Chewy. Let's meet some people," I replied.

At home, Holly and Annie were weeding in the garden, getting all in order for the summer renters. When I walked through the gate with Chewy, Annie's immediate response was, "Oh no, you don't!" Annie wanted to properly mourn Opie and at least wait through the summer before getting another dog.

"Just for one night?" I asked. "I'll take her back tomorrow." I let her off the leash, and she circled the yard, tail down, head down, nervous. She'd been penned up for a long time. I worried she'd run away or turn nasty. We all sat and watched. Eventually, she completed her rounds and returned to me. She took the leash in her mouth, wagged her tail, and said with her eyes, "I am your friend. I am the one you've been looking for." Then she laid her head on my shoulder. Annie gasped. "What have they been training those dogs to do over at ARF?" she said, but she was laughing.

That evening, Chewy went with us to two lawn parties. At one she fetched the host's newspaper for him. At another she bounded around the lawn with such glee that the hostess was alarmed for her wine glasses and trays of crudités. "That dog is not trained!" she screeched.

I took Chewy home, glad to be free of the East Hampton summer inanities and soon off to Maine. Could she stay?

First we had a family discussion. At breakfast Chewy was the quintessential diplomat, making the rounds of the table, her head on our knees, looking at each of us with her deep, kind eyes. Never begging for food. Chewy never begged for anything.

Yes, we voted. She could stay. But that name. Did she chew up stuff as a puppy? Was that still her hidden fault? In any case, "Chewy" didn't fit.

"How about Louie?" I suggested. Louie sounded like Chewy, and she might be more comfortable with it.

"She's a girl, Dad," Holly reminded me.

"A single mom," Annie added.

"How about Floozy?" I tried.

"Not funny, Dad."

"I know," said Annie. "My favorite comic book character. Lulu. Little Lulu."

So it was– Chewy to Louie to Lulu, which didn't fit her either, but it avoided a radical change in her name.

Within days, Lulu and I were off to Maine to open up the cabin for the summer and finish work on the tower. Annie and Holly stayed down in East Hampton until school was out. Lulu was a wonderful car companion, alert and watchful as we negotiated the long concrete drive to Sedgwick and the tower, which I hoped still stood.

Sedgwick is at the unspoiled southern tip of a peninsula that extends into the Atlantic Ocean, bordered on the west by the Penobscot River, which drains much of upstate Maine, and on the east by Blue Hill Bay.

Once you have traveled on consumer-devoured and consumer-devouring U.S. Route 1 and have turned onto the peninsula, you are in a different country. You will know you have arrived there because people wave to each other and to strangers as they pass.

Sedgwick village is about eight miles from E. B. White's farm in Brooklin. You reach Sedgwick from Brooklin by crossing the Benjamin River on a rocky causeway. The river joins Eggemoggin Reach at Sedgwick Harbor.

There's a simple pontoon dock on that small harbor,

and in the summertime kids fish from the dock and swim in the water, which rarely gets higher than fifty-five degrees, except for maybe two weeks at the end of August. Perfect for Lulu, who loved to swim.

The sun washes the land and water of this whole peninsula with a pale yellow light, and the sky is constantly and brilliantly changing like a slow-motion kaleidoscope.

Sedgwick village has a post office, a library that opens a few hours a week, a general store (alas, no longer), and a half-dozen houses at the river bend that are painted the very un-Maine colors of chartreuse, mauve, and tan. There's the gold-domed Baptist church, several artists' studios, and a carpenter's shop in a garage attached to the carpenter's house, plus a small antique shop, and the home of a lady who sells "fine hand-knit sweaters," which she makes right there. Later, Grammy-winning musician and composer Paul Sullivan set up his recording studio in a house overlooking the river, and later still, I opened the miniscule summertime Pushcart bookstore in a one-room-and-porch structure behind the antique store. "The world's smallest bookstore" is our claim.

Sedgwick village is this sort of place: At about six one morning, a stranger still to this community, I stopped in at the general store to buy a fresh blueberry muffin and coffee from Gretchen, the owner. I sat on the hood of my car with Lulu near the causeway as the sun rose behind me and a woman and a young boy led a procession over the river: four huge, clomping workhorses and a happy mutt on their way to a field for the horses' breakfast, I guessed.

"Hi!" called the woman to the stranger sitting on his car hood, with his shaggy pal, eating a muffin in the early light.

"Good morning!" I waved, moved by her simple greeting. In East Hampton we see no such processions, and strangers on car hoods at 6:00 A.M. are regarded with suspicion.

Not many tourists pass through Sedgwick village. Most of them take the turnoff at Route 15 a few miles to the west, a more direct route to Blue Hill or busy strip-mall-crazed Ellsworth. Its more direct line saves them five minutes. For what? I don't know. The slow and steady pace of the woman, the boy, the horses, and the mutt is not valued in the age of speed and the info super-highway, our current fake gods.

Because of this pace, many residents of this peninsula live decades longer than people from "away," despite a climate that can be brutal, especially in winter. As the Maine poet Edwin Arlington Robinson wrote, "Maine is where children learn to walk on frozen toes."

E. B. White endured more than fifty winters here. In a letter from his farm, he wrote, "About ten days ago we had a tremendous gale. Our power was gone most of the night, trees went down, and the Deer Isle Bridge pulled a tendon. It's a lofty bridge, and when it gets slatting around in high wind it seems to lose its cool."

The terrific winter winds may be why Down East, Maine, is not known for its towers. I approached Christy Hill with trepidation, worried that I would find my creation flattened by storms.

But the tower still stood. It had resisted the winter wind bravely, still covered in its Christo wrap. I got to work on the clapboard siding and interior trim.

When not on tower duties, Lulu and I headed out into bear country.

Farley Mowat, in his dog memoir, *The Dog Who Wouldn't Be*, about his mutt called "Mutt," states of the great plains of western Canada, "The prairies could be only half real to a boy without a dog." That's how it was for me with Lulu in our Maine wilderness.

Bear country was everywhere around us– miles and miles of it. Big, old black bears rolled in the summertime blueberry fields out back scooping up paws of berries; they fled in terror when Lulu trotted down the road (hunters used dogs to chase bears– why hunt bears? To kill a big thing, that's why, stupid). Lulu would have preferred to play with the bears, but they weren't that silly.

Still they didn't like to be surprised. Moms with cubs could be very nasty. So on our daily four-mile hike down to the post office and back, I would have loud conversations with Lulu, or I would sometimes sing to warn the bears that we were about. Lulu and I would return with our mail, rest halfway on a blueberry knoll and check out the clouds, the sun, or the fog, swatting some flies, and head on back up the hill, talking and singing. Once a bear crossed the road, apparently not hearing our approach. He regarded us and silently hurried off. Lulu wished he had stayed.

One day at the top of the hill while waiting for Lulu to pee, I looked into a deep ditch and saw a huge bear seemingly asleep, his back up against a tree, head lolling as if drunk or hung over. We left. They next day he was still there, dead for sure. Hit by a car, said the game warden later, but I suspected he'd been shot for kicks.

The Frost Pond was our secret adventure many summer afternoons. (In Maine lakes are called ponds, with typical Down East understatement.) Even some locals knew nothing of this pure lake hidden away down a rough dirt road, lost in woods and blueberry fields. On our hikes there, Lulu and I met only eagles and turkeys and deer and now and then a coyote or a porcupine, which Lulu was wise enough to avoid. The pond was her huge pleasure. She'd dive off the bank into the clear water and watch me with delighted eyes, paddling herself cool.

When she was still young enough, we'd head off deeper into the woods, marking our return trail with bits of paper, having no compass or other sensible gear that any Boy Scout would pack. The woods were laced with old logging trails. We followed them here and there singing out for the bears (and more dangerous, a mad moose). My favorite tune, for some reason, was from Disney's *Snow White*, the dwarfs' "Whistle While You Work." Whistling and singing, we covered many miles. Our grand discovery was an ancient eight-mile walking trail from the tower to the old ferry dock at the Reach, a dock abandoned in 1938 when the Deer Isle Bridge was built by FDR's "work projects" laborers.

Lulu and I were making up for all the years since Duke and I had to surrender our pathetic suburban wilderness to developers. It seemed to me that nothing could ever ruin Sedgwick; there was simply too much of it. New houses sprouted up here and there, but many old houses were likely to go unclaimed and collapse into their cellar holes, where nature embraced them again.

Sedgwick existed in a steady state. Our insane national infatuation with growth at all costs didn't apply here. The GDP was at slack tide in Sedgwick.

The blueberry fields that surrounded the tower had been nurtured and raked for hundreds of years. The streams ran pure; the rough gravel and stone beaches were unspoiled by the tourists; and the village looked the same as it had for centuries.

Lulu and I imagined that this was truly home.

In the evenings, before she became too old, Lulu chased tennis balls up and down the dirt road in front of the tower. Then I sipped some wine, and we sat next to each other in the tall grass and felt twilight descend around us.

We talked in silence. If I was depressed for some reason, she sat beside me and licked my hand. "Thanks, Lulu," I'd say and know it was all better for now.

In *Dog Years*, Mark Doty recalls such moments with his beloved Mr. Beau:

> *When I adopted him, he was a neglected slip of a thing, but his heart was capable of soaring. I call on his spirit when things get logy, when I feel an internal clock slipping into what Dickinson called an "hour of lead." Attention to the mortal shadowing of all beauty – that's a perspective that comes to me too easily, something I have to resist. And that's why I loved that heavy golden paw tapping at my knee* – notice me, come back. *A kind of sweet slap, with the blunt tips of his nails poking at me. A slap I miss now with all my heart.*

For our early morning ritual, Lulu and I walked back to a rock outcropping that Holly and I had unearthed near the tower – a low bolder shaped roughly like a heart and cracked in two. A sacred spot, I thought. For now Lulu and I watched the sun rise out of the ocean, my arm around her, no words necessary. Our new day was beginning, "Like the first morning," as the hymn says.

Later, Lulu and I would build a chapel here, I imagined. We began to scout for stones for that chapel.

🙠 And then, one winter Max arrived. He stayed off and on for six years. Max was a high-class, purebred, son of champions golden retriever. His owners were new friends we'd met in East Hampton who were about to spend their first summer in Maine and wanted information on life up north. Annie, Holly, and I were invited for dinner, and there we met Max, the family dog. It was love at first sight for Annie. Max seemed delighted to meet her. He stuck by her throughout the evening, putting his head in her lap and nudging her for pats on the head. She was enchanted.

That summer our two families, including dogs, met often for suppers and picnics. Often Annie would stop by their house going to or from shopping in Blue Hill ostensibly for a visit– more likely to have a cuddle with Max.

Late in the summer on a lawn sweeping down to the harbor– a party, a few drinks, Max romping about– our hostess said, "We're looking for a home for Max this winter. Just during the week. We're moving back to the city so our son can go to school there. I've put an ad in the *East Hampton Star*, but if you know of anyone– "

Annie burst out, "We'll take him!" And that was that.

All fall and winter Max was ours during the week. He was his owners' on the weekends, except when they went skiing or sailing in the Caribbean or in the spring when their son had sports or any one of a dozen reasons for them not to come out to East Hampton– then he was ours. One glorious year, our friends decided to move to Barcelona, and Max moved in full-time, but when they came back we resumed the routine.

Max was never really our dog, but Annie and he adored each other. Every winter morning they would go for a walk on the bay beaches along the dunes and grass, Max always about twenty feet ahead and stopping every few minutes to look back at her and smile his enormous smile. "Aren't we having fun?" he'd laugh, like Merle. "Yes!" Annie said, laughing back.

Max was one happy dog. Even as he was shuttled back and forth between our house and his peripatetic owners, he'd laugh and laugh. Annie declared he was all love – pure and simple love covered over in a big coat of golden fur. We had at that time five cats, plus Lulu, Holly's friends coming and going, many parties, delivery men, houseguests (some with their own dogs) – nothing seemed to faze him. A bark of greeting, a wagging tail. His favorite trick was to sneak under the dining room table during dinner parties and, with the stealth and precision of an espionage agent, delicately remove each guest's napkin from their laps. He would roll over in an ecstasy of delight when his trick was discovered, a pile of shredded napkins at his feet.

He was the kindest dog I ever met. On gray winter days, Max would ride with Lulu and me – she, curled up in the passenger seat beside me; he, when I looked in the rearview mirror, in back with the biggest grin on his face. "Isn't this fun?" he'd say. Yes, it always was.

Max and Lulu were beach buddies – but each knew its territory. Lulu owned me, Max owned Annie. They never squabbled or growled. For years, they slept on the floor next to our bed, never in it, and were the most peaceful of friends.

Two weeks before Max died, Annie remembers sitting on the East Hampton beach with him. Holly was off at school, and we were both feeling a bit empty. This particular beach is on the bay surrounded by a nature preserve and at one end meets an inlet leading from the bay into Three Mile Harbor. Across the bay you can see the outline of Long Island, and beyond that is Connecticut. This was a favorite spot for Annie and Max, and on this particular day Annie gave him a hug. "Max, you are my best friend," she declared and meant it. Max smiled back that she was his best friend too.

Then he was gone. He and Lulu had torn up the beach one early spring evening and were exhausted from racing in and out of the shallow water. They both jumped into the station wagon, and when we got home, both jumped out. Only when Max landed, he collapsed. He could not walk. His hind legs were seemingly paralyzed. Annie and I fashioned a stretcher out of a rug and carried him into the house. On the phone, the vet asked if he seemed in pain. No, he didn't. Only puzzled. Why couldn't he move? The vet said to call him if anything changed and to bring him in the next morning. We petted Max through the night.

The vet said he would never walk again. He had suffered a sort of stroke – not to his brain but to his hindquarters. There was nothing they could do. We talked to his owners in New York about fixing him up with a little wheeled cart for his legs so he could still get around, but we were really just stalling for time. Max, who was all joy and bounce at his advanced age, would have been miserable, we agreed– peeing and soiling himself, an invalid.

So after days of agonizing discussions, Annie and I sat with him as the vet prepared the needle. Max rested his head on Annie's knee and with a nudge asked her to pet his head. She did as he slipped under.

A few years back, the memoir I had written about building the tower on Christy Hill attracted a flattering round of publicity, and I was asked to pose on a small balcony on the upper floor for a photo, which would run with the *New York Times* feature. Below, Max lay snoozing on a large, sun-soaked flat rock. The *Times* photographer recognized a photo op when he had one, but would the dog stay put while I scrambled up into the tower and he set up his gear? Max lifted his head, smiled, and stretched out again in a languid pose, perfect for the shoot.

We scattered his ashes around that rock. Annie and Holly fashioned a tombstone there: "Here lies Max, a golden dog with a golden heart."

For this book I asked Annie what she recalled most about Max. "He gave me such a gift," she said. "I'm not quite sure even now what it was. He reached a place in me I'd never visited, and he made it our little spot where only he and I went. I never knew I had within me that place."

⤳ Summer to summer, with Holly often at camp or at school, Lulu and I were kids together. And summer to summer, without really noticing it, we grew old together. I built a cottage near the tower on concrete pillars to replace the Deer Isle cabin we had sold for Holly's college tuition. The heat began to get to aging Lulu, and she hid under the cottage many July days. Our trips to the post office and to the Pushcart bookstore were more often by Oldsmobile than foot. We also drove halfway to the Frost Pond and sometimes merely climbed a nearby hill there to worship Acadia Park's mountains and the sea together. Hands out and palms open, I blessed those mountains and gently stirring ocean, and Lulu and I were blessed in return.

To the very end– winter or summer– Lulu loved the water. Her great joy was a robust splash, even into icy slush, as she retrieved a stick or a ball. Time and time again she'd ask for another toss, and I'd have to stop before she exhausted herself. On hot summer days, if I walked down the hill to the bookstore or post office, I'd often try to sneak through the woods and leave her behind, fearful of the heat. But she'd always hear a leaf rustle or a twig snap, and she'd bound from under the house, ready to roll.

Lulu was somewhere near eleven or twelve, and I was well into my sixth decade. Our whiskers were turning gray and then white, our bellies filling out.

When Lulu was diagnosed with breast cancer– about the same time I was– some friends, including my oncologist, found my depression over her dying hard to understand. My cancer I could deal with, not Lulu's. It's just a dog, I heard in their muted sympathy.

My friend Rob McCall, the Congregational minister in Blue Hill, understood about Lulu and me, about our perfect wordless conversations.

"Lulu and I talk about important stuff: about running on blueberry fields, the weather, chasing sticks and balls, and food. Lulu loves to eat. She eats just about anything, unfortunately."

"I'm sure you don't talk about theology, then." Rob laughed.

"Nope, just the important stuff."

Rob knew there was no need for theology with Lulu. She was unconditional love, dog as god spelled backward. A cliché, I know, but the sentiment survives because it has always been true.

Our last hike in Maine was into a gold October valley, over maroon blueberry fields to the Frost Pond. Lulu swam, and I just lay on the field and watched the clear sun-washed sky and wondered if anything would ever be this perfect again.

Lying in that field, I remembered St. Francis's hymn, "Canticle of the Creatures" or "The Song of Brother Sun," a vision of nature quite unlike that of his gloomy church. During his last days, suffering in his dark cell in Portiuncula, Francis summoned the brothers to listen to his final composition:

> *Praised by you, my Lord, with all your creatures*
> *especially Sir Brother sun*
> *through whom you give us the day and light*
> *he is beautiful, radiant with great splendor,*
> *and of you, most High, he is our symbol . . .*

The spirit of St. Francis was with Lulu and me in those final months — old dog, aging man, chasing up and down hills and beaches for the sheer waning exuberance of it all.

One morning, only a few days before my first surgery,

as I waited in East Hampton for the trip to New York's Memorial Sloan-Kettering, St. Francis may have visited us in a more direct way. Lulu slept on the floor while I lay on the sunroom sofa, tired, weak, apprehensive. Paul Sullivan, my friend from Sedgwick, telephoned to wish me well and said that Reverend McCall had mentioned my name on the Sunday prayer list. After we said good-bye, the room filled with what I can only describe as a force, as if the air pressure had tripled. It wasn't a vision of light and love but a sensation of universal power. I skeptically tried to explain it away as a mood of the moment brought on by the phone call but couldn't, and although I expected it to fade away immediately – and begged it not to – the presence lingered with me and Lulu for perhaps half an hour before gradually leaving.

It is easy to dismiss such accounts. We have read endless tales of Jesus or Mary or a saint appearing to true believers in a pizza pie crust or a wallpaper stain. But I cannot deny that force. It was unexpected and not requested. I needed comfort and assurance, not force. But force I got. Nothing gentle about it.

One of the most convincing spiritual visitations is that of novelist Reynolds Price in his classic memoir of cancer recovery, *A Whole New Life*. Price's cancer, unlike mine, was exceedingly painful, a tumor that curled down his spine like a snake. He endured months of radiation therapy.

One morning, Price says, he fell into an exhausted sleep. He was transported to the Sea of Galilee. Jesus came toward him. Price called out to him about his pain and chances for survival. Jesus said merely, "Your sins are forgiven," and turned and walked away. Price complained to himself that his sins are not exactly what bothered him at the moment. He asked Jesus about ending the pain, and would he live? Jesus said simply, "That too." And Price finds himself back in his room.

He did indeed survive, confined to a wheelchair. And he learned to manage his pain.

Price is quick to criticize his memory of this event. As a respected literary critic and essayist, he won't accept this as a piece of Hallmark card sentimentality. Perhaps his pain had driven him over the edge? No, he answers, his visit was real. Jesus did speak those six words. Not a vision, not a metaphor, not wishful thinking, not temporary insanity. No question. Real.

In the same way, I cannot question the force in my room— St. Francis, Jesus, the Holy Spirit, none of the above— it makes no difference. Something else had been with my dying dog and me that afternoon. I long for it to return.

Just after my surgery, I noticed that Lulu's chest on the right side had developed a mass— about the size of a child's football. A fatty deposit, I hoped. But it grew larger, and Lulu began to slow down. No longer did she lead our beach walks but lagged behind. And soon she couldn't swim for a stick; she just walked into the water and stood there, grateful for her old ocean friend, as if lost in nostalgia.

I took her to the vet, who did a biopsy and put her on antibiotics to bring down a slight fever. I said I suspected she had cancer. When I mentioned my own recent breast cancer operation, he remarked that it was not unusual for a pet and owner to develop the same disease.

Weeks later biopsy results and X-rays confirmed Lulu's

massive tumor and another in her abdomen. Nothing could be done. "We can ease the pain for a few weeks. That's all, unfortunately," said the vet.

Lulu wanted to die alone and hidden. Twice she ran off into the night after I had let her out to pee.

The first time, when she didn't respond to my constant call, I worried that she had found a hole or shed to do her dying in, but at 2:00 A.M., suddenly she was standing outside the door, too weak to bark or scratch. I let her in with cries of welcome for a friend resurrected.

For a few days she showed signs of recovery, scrambling into the car for rides to the beach, eating with customary vacuum-cleaner lust. But on the night of a March snowstorm, three days before she died, she again ran off into the woods and ignored my calls. After midnight, Annie was shutting off the lights when she spotted Lulu standing in the snow motionless, coated with ice, a white ghost. Again we welcomed her back as if resurrected. But in the nights ahead she could not sleep, panting constantly and moving from spot to spot every few minutes because of her pain.

On March 10, the date my father died, I took Lulu for her last trip to the vet, still uncertain about what to do. The vet said it was time. Lulu didn't notice the injection into her rump. She quietly lay down on a quilt while the doctor, nurse, and I patted her and told her how very loved she was.

Her death hit me like a horrible physical pain. I barely made it out of the vet's office, and on the way home I became a sobbing road menace.

For weeks, unable to endure my dogless state, I searched for a dog with Lulu's eyes. One day Holly, home from school, spotted an ARF listing in the newspaper and said, "Look at this dog's eyes, Dad, so kind."

I adopted that dog, a border collie mix with energy like a living spark. I named her St. Francis of Assisi – Franny.

In the spring, Franny and I returned to Maine and the Frost Pond. I scattered Lulu's ashes along the shore of our last perfect day.

From Trixie to Lulu and beyond, my dogs had guided me on a spiritual sojourn. They were fearless champions of faith – faith in each other, faith in the Great Spirit that lives in each of us. Lulu opened that final door for me, total openness and trust between God's creatures. Perhaps only dogs in their innocence can teach us that.

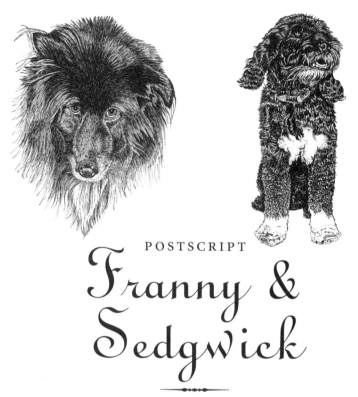

# Franny & Sedgwick

*In the midst of winter, I finally learned that there
was in me an invincible summer.*
ALBERT CAMUS

IN THE SUMMERS since Lulu died, I have struggled with
recurring cancer – more operations, chemo, radiation,
the usual procession. At times I endured Emily Dickin-
son's "hour of lead" – moments when I was tempted to
walk into the frozen bay and end it. So far I live and
thrive, and Annie, Holly, Franny, and Sedgwick do too.

Sedgwick is a new Portuguese water dog – a Christmas
puppy for Annie. Holly had been begging Annie to get

another dog to replace Max, but though Annie went with her to ARF on a number of occasions, nothing seemed to click. I first met the breed, favored by the late Senator Edward Kennedy (Sunny and Splash) and later by President Obama's family (Bo), one afternoon on the beach. That Porty (as they are called) seemed an ideal dog, and his owner was quick to agree. He praised Porties as intelligent, affectionate, energetic, devoted to owners, hair instead of fur so does not shed . . . I listened and admired, but what I saw was the dog who could finally replace Max in Annie's heart.

Our Sedgwick has no papers, no lofty lineage. He's an accident – a moment of abandon by two Porties on a Bellport, Long Island lawn while their owners frolicked in a hot tub out back. I saw an ad in *Newsday* a few days before Christmas, and Holly and I bought him for a bargain price. We put a big red bow around his neck and presented a small, curly-haired, black puppy with white paws that looked like socks and a white bowtie on his chest to the surprised Annie.

The pup was the high point of an otherwise low holiday. I was deep into cancer treatment at Sloan-Kettering with a third recurrence and was sure I was not going to make it out of the long winter months. In Maine they talk about "the March hump." So many of the elderly or sick don't make it beyond the still icy conditions of March into the spring. We named this ebullient and healing bundle of energy "Sedgwick" for the place I loved most on earth. His nonstop kisses that winter may have saved my life.

Perhaps someday I will write of Franny and Sedgwick but not now. Our story is still to be lived. They lie at my feet, regarding me anxiously, desperate to be off on a walk with Annie, Holly, and me, tired of my scribbling on this clipboard with a Bic pen. Young Sedgwick knows that such pens are more useful for chewing.

Over the years, with Annie's and Holly's occasional help, I have constructed a stone chapel in the woods where Lulu and I sat on our sacred, brokenhearted boulder. The chapel, fashioned from random rocks, endures as a monument to Lulu, Max, Opie, Charlie, Airport, Sophie, Rocky, Ellen, The Mayor of Bridgehampton, Snopes, Earl, Duke, and Trixie– and our current canine friends who remind me with mounting frustration that it is time for a family hike across the blueberry fields and a dip in the pure Maine water.

*All knowledge, the totality of all questions and all answers is contained in the dog.*
FRANZ KAFKA

BILL HENDERSON is founder of Pushcart Press and editor and publisher of the annual *Pushcart Prize: Best of the Small Presses*, now in its thirty-fifth year. He is the author of the memoirs *His Son* (Norton, 1981), *Her Father* (Faber and Faber, 1995), *Tower* (Farrar, Straus & Giroux, 2000), and *Simple Gifts* (Free Press, 2006). He received the 2006 *Poets & Writers* / Barnes & Noble "Writers for Writers" citation and the 2006 Lifetime Achievement Award from the National Book Critics Circle.

LESLIE MOORE draws portraits of dogs for many owners (and breeds). She was a favorite artist of the late Senator Edward Kennedy and drew his beloved Portuguese waterdogs Sunny and Splash as well as his wooden schooner *Mya*. She drew many of the dogs in this memoir from photos of Bill Henderson's dogs.

A NOTE ON THE TYPE

The text of this book was set in Minion, a word that not only refers to a size of type but also is defined (appropriately enough) as "faithful companion." Minion was designed by Robert Slimbach for Adobe Systems in 1990. In Slimbach's own words, "I like to think of Minion as a synthesis of historical and contemporary elements. My intention with the design was to make a progressive Aldine style text family that is both stylistically distinctive and utilitarian. The design grew out of my formal calligraphy, written in the Aldine style. By adapting my hand lettering to the practical concerns of computer aided text typeface design, I hoped to design a fresh interpretation of a classical alphabet." The display face used for chapter openings is Linoleah designed by Morris Fuller Benton in 1905. Linoleah is reminiscent of handwriting found in early twentieth-century school books and diaries.

*Design by Sara Eisenman*